A JOURNEY OF
FRIENDSHIP

A Thru-Hike on the Appalachian Trail

Bruce,
DREAM IT—DO IT!
Melody :)

Melody A. Blaney and L.K. Ullyart
(Midnite & Out of Africa)

The following trademarks appear throughout this book: Gregory, Backpacker, Eureka, Sierra Designs, Moonstone, Slumberjack, First Ascent, Sweetwater, Scorpion, MSR, Vasque, Hi-Tec, Asolo, Gore-Tex, Ridgerest, Therm-a-Rest, Duofold, Marmot, Patagonia, Swiss Army, Lipton, Little Debbie, Mountain Dew, M & M, Milky Way, Pop Tarts, Nutri Grain, Kool-Aid, Crystal Light.

First printing 1997
Printed by The River Press
Marietta, OH 45750

Blaney, Melody & Ullyart, L.K.
    A Journey of Friendship, A Thru-Hike on the
    Appalachian Trail

ISBN 0-9657740-0-7

TO MY FAMILY

*Who have always believed in me and stood
by me no matter what path I have taken,
and to the memory of my dear friend
Joella, I lived for you.*

Melody (Midnite)

INTRODUCTION

Midnite

From the beginning, I never said that I <u>would</u> thru-hike the 2,159 mile Appalachian Trail, only that I would try it. Every obstacle that we overcame: climbing rocks, fording streams, dealing with endless days of rain, and walking in pain, prepared us for another leg of our journey and our ultimate goal, Mt. Katahdin. This hike was the most difficult and glorious experience of my life and I would not have changed one moment of it, be it, good or bad. I never would have attempted or completed such an undertaking without the help of God, my family, and of course, Out of Africa. They were always by my side, helping me to carry my load.

Out of Africa

The trail was a glorious adventure and although it had it's ups and downs, I would gladly do it all again. My hiking partner was a continual source of laughter, inspiration and motivation to me. With her help, Mt. Katahdin became a reality.

All glory comes from daring to begin

AUTHOR'S NOTE

A Journey of Friendship is both the story of two friends and a partial biography. Generally, in the pages that follow, the two of us, Mel and Lindi, speak as one - about what we have jointly experienced and recall. Occasionally, however, there are points in the narrative where it becomes necessary to abandon the collective "we" and to present the events at hand from the point of view of one or the other of us. The reasons for this should be clear from the context.

CHAPTER 1

WAYAH BALD, APRIL 15, 1996

The overcast morning had eventually turned to rain and by early afternoon a cold heavy rain was falling. It hung around us like a heavy gray curtain, and within minutes we were soaked through to our skin. Up until then we had just been walking together. On Wayah Bald we would begin hiking together as partners.

Wayah Mountain stands at an elevation of 5,000 feet and the only two buildings are the lookout tower and two roomy brick built toilets, big enough, we thought, to spend the night in. The alternative was for both of us to sleep in Midnite's tent. Before Fontana Dam we had only one tent and while Midnite's tent was ample for her and her pack it would be a tight squeeze for two of us plus our packs, but we had grown tired of the crowded shelters and decided that for one night we could survive with both of us in one tent; so we pushed on to our planned campsite. Wet and tired we hastily pitched the tent, and while Midnite figured out the best way to pack both us and our packs into what is basically a one person and one pack tent, Out of Africa collected water. We ate a quick supper under a dripping pine tree before throwing two soaked packs and two wet and tired bodies into our home for the evening. "Someday," Midnite said, "We'll laugh about this!" As we drifted off to sleep, legs stretched out over each other, we figured that by morning the weather conditions would improve.

The first sounds of morning were the patter of rain drops on the rain fly and as we emerged awkwardly from the tent, we were dismayed to see that it wasn't rain, but ice and snow, and the ground was already covered with white. Our bandanas which had been tied to a tree the night before were frozen solid, and our water bags left outside the tent had suffered a similar fate. Our prediction was wrong, it had gotten worse.

The journey of a thousand miles begins with one step

Something as simple as stuffing the tent into a stuff sack or clipping the hip belt on our packs became difficult with our fingers numb from the cold. But we worked together as a team to break camp and anxiously started walking to generate body heat. As the sun warmed the frozen trees we were pelted with ice from them and soon shed our layers of clothing. It turned out to be a glorious day and it seemed we were walking through a magical wonderland. Everywhere we looked was frosted white and the sun glinted off the trees and bushes. We soon learned that the rigors of the day before were easily forgotten when we were faced with a new day. We hiked our biggest day of 16 miles since we left Springer Mountain on April 5th.

The experience of that unforgettable night bonded our partnership that would carry us 2,159 miles to Mt. Katahdin, Maine and the northern terminus of the Appalachian Trail.

Our friendship had started eight months ago when Lindi answered an ad for a hiking partner to thru-hike the Appalachian Trail that Mel had placed in the Appalachian Trailway News. We had corresponded with each other initially by letters from Mel in Marietta, Ohio, and Lindi in Cape Town, South Africa, but as the time grew closer for us to meet, we became impatient with the length of time for letters to reach us and relied on electronic mail and Fax machines to communicate. We met for the first time 11 days prior to Wayah Bald at a hostel in Atlanta.

Mel: *My trip to Atlanta from Ohio seemed to take forever as I traveled in the van with my family. I had decided in July of 1995 (after months of thinking about it) that the time was right for me to do the trail. I placed my house on the market and when it sold in three days I knew it was meant to be. From that time forward every waking moment was spent preparing for the trail - physically and mentally. My lists had lists as I figured out what I would need for my maildrops, how much money it would take, and how I spent many late nights figuring mileage and town visits to pull it all together. Most of my essential gear had been purchased over the last two years as my love of backpacking grew, so the only thing left to do was find a partner to share my dream. I received many responses to the ad I had* placed in the *Appalachian Trailway News*, but when I received Lindi's first letter and she said, "I'm the partner for you," I knew my search was over.

Friends constantly asked me before I left what I would do if Lindi and I didn't get along. That thought never entered my mind. Her letters over the months revealed we both had the same hopes and dreams for a thru-hike and my gut feeling (something I have always relied on) told me it would work. I already had a great deal of respect for Lindi because she left her job, boyfriend, and home and flew halfway across the world to pursue a dream that could end the first day out with the twist of an ankle.

I phoned Lindi from the motel in Gainesville and couldn't believe that after all these months I was speaking to her for the first time. I arranged to pick her up at a hostel in Atlanta the next day and was so anxious to meet her that we arrived an hour earlier than planned. The staff at the hostel couldn't locate her and my sister and I checked restaurants and a tea room (she's British - where else would she be?) across the street, but couldn't find her. Returning to the hostel I decided we would wait (I would pace) outside in the garden until the arranged meeting time. Not knowing what she looked like I anxiously eyed everyone coming and going looking for someone with a backpack and soon she appeared with her red pack in tow. As first meetings often are, I felt awkward and wanted to hug her and say "Let's go hike," but instead jammed my hands into my pockets and for the first time in my life was at a loss for words. Soon the talk turned to our journey and I felt as if we had been friends forever.

Back at the motel in Gainesville, I took a long hot bath and wrote in my journal, as I did religiously every night, and tried to relax and unwind from the excitement of the day. I slept very little as I went over in my mind all the last minute details of my pack and wondered what Lindi thought of her first day in the states as well as her partner. Up to this point, her vision of me and our impending hike had been formed by the written words in my letters. The next morning I was more than ready to go when I carried my pack to the parking lot of the motel and was surprised to see Lindi standing there looking more like a model with her red lipstick on, than someone who was about to set off on a 2,159 mile hike.

Lindi: I had just returned from visiting my mother in England and my friend Des held out an airmail envelope to me. "It's from Melody" he said. I gave it back to him, "You open it." Months later when I told Mel that she smiled."Why didn't you want to open it," she asked. It was a hard question to answer - maybe, I thought, that if Des opened it it would be good news. It was anyway. I had decided to hike the trail three years earlier after reading an article in the National Geographic. It was something that I just had to do. The ultimate trail, I thought. I liked Mel's ad - "to experience all the trail has to offer." I liked the idea of seeing the real America, the real people and the real towns. Not the people and towns that you see as a tourist.

Des slit the envelope neatly and unfolded the paper. He scanned it quickly and handed it to me. "It's ok," he said, "She wants you!" I took the page from him and read it quickly, she indeed did want me. I remember I had written "I'm the partner for you" and as soon as I had read her ad, I knew that's what I was. I began to make plans.

My backpack is South African manufactured, and a relatively simple design. Des bought my sleeping bag for me and my imported Therm-a-rest mattress. Although I had taken my sleeping bag with me on hiking trips in South Africa, I had never needed to use it to keep warm. I would just lie on the top and really had no experience of how to use a sleeping bag in cold weather. On the first night out it got really cold and I crawled into my bag with all my clothes on - including my jacket! I thought I would die of cold. Mel told me to take all my clothes off and let my body heat warm my bag up. I thought she was mad, but I did as she suggested and was surprised on how warm I was. I then worked out how to pull the hood around my head and draw up the strings around my neck. After that I was very warm all the time, even in the coldest weather.

I bought myself an imported MSR International WhisperLite stove and practiced with it every opportunity I got. I already had a new pair of Hi-Tec hiking boots and decided to take them and if I needed another pair I would buy them in America. Apart from a few small items, that was the extent of what I could buy in South Africa. I knew I would need rain pants and a hiking jacket but decided to wait as I expected that there would be a better selection in the states. I had no idea about cold weather underwear. I had never even heard of polypropylene!

With Des supporting me all the way, I gave up my job as a graphic artist and headed for America. Des even bought my air ticket for me. I landed in Atlanta on April 3rd, 1996 and went to the International Hostel in Atlanta where Mel and her family were to meet me. It had been a long flight. From South Africa to Amsterdam, and from Amsterdam to Atlanta - 23 hours. I was tired and I slept for ten hours at the hostel.

The next morning I got my things together and prepared myself for my first meeting with my hiking partner. Unknown to me, they were already there and had been looking for me. Somehow we eluded each other and they decided to wait for me in the garden. I had the same thought. When I got there I saw all these people and didn't really want to go and sit in the middle of them to wait for my partner. Just as I turned away, I heard someone say "Lindi." That was our first meeting. I had thought that I would hug her, but I was too shy. I don't even think we shook hands. Mel's whole family, with the exception of her brother Stephen and brother-in-law Terry, were there.

They had driven from Marietta, Ohio in Mel's sister's van and they had a banner which read "Maine or Bust" written across it. This was our support team. We drove to Gainesville and stayed overnight in a motel. I had to go shopping to buy seven days of food. It was like Aladdin's cave to me with the vast amount of foods that are available in America. By 10:00 that night I had sorted my food and was packed and ready to go - I hoped! I hardly slept that night and was wide awake at 3:30 and lay waiting to get up. We were up at 5:00 a.m. and ready to go by 6:30 on a cold clear morning. This was it. After breakfast we drove to Amicalola Falls State Park and the start of our journey. (I should add, that I never wore lipstick on the trail, and didn't carry any with me!)

It was a bit of an ordeal for me meeting all these new friends as I'm basically a shy person. I wondered what Mel thought of me - I remember thinking "She must be wondering what she has got herself in to." Everyone was talking and I found myself frantically searching for something to say! After our chatty letters, Mel must have thought me really odd. I soon realized though, that Mel and her family were very special and treated me like a member of the family. By the time we got to Whitley Shelter on the trail I knew I had to come out of my shell. Everyone was so loud and confident and I was in danger of fading away, so I thought if you can't beat them, join them. Over the weeks and months my confidence grew until I got to the stage where I could sing a duet with Mel with complete confidence.

The anticipation of what would lie ahead of us on our journey increased as we were driven by Mel's family to Amicalola Falls State Park in Georgia, but some tension was relieved as we weighed our backpacks at the Ranger Station. Mel had hoped to start out with a pack weight of 50 pounds and punched the air, with a joyous yelp of "Yes" when it tipped the scales at a reasonable 45 pounds. Lindi had no idea what her pack would weigh and nodded happily at a mere 37 pounds.

We had read that the approach trail to Springer Mountain, the southern terminus of the trail, was someone's idea of a cruel joke and that since it is not officially part of the Appalachian Trail (A.T.) we decided not to put ourselves through the abuse of a difficult eight miles BEFORE we started our hike. We instead drove a mile north of the terminus which meant that we had to hike south to reach the actual starting point of the trail we had both been dreaming of.

The months of planning were over and the tearful good-byes had been said to Mel's family. We had added our sentiments to the sign-in register as we stood before the bronze plaque, the symbol of the start of the trail. We each collected a stone that would accompany us (we hoped) to our destination of Mount Katahdin, Maine. Before taking our first of five million steps, Mel bent down to kiss the plaque and promised the next sign she would kiss would be atop Katahdin.

The fog that had been with us since morning had lifted and the sun was shining down on us as we shouldered our packs and began to walk. So many emotions ran through our heads; fear, excitement, anticipation and we decided to set small goals for ourselves rather than look at all 2,159 miles of the trail. Our first goal would be Fontana Dam, North Carolina, 161 miles away and Mel's first of eleven maildrops. Mel had prepared boxes of supplies to be mailed by her parents to her at towns along the trail that we would pass, approximately every two weeks or every 150 miles. It was impossible for Lindi to do the same so she relied on re-supplying in towns. Mel started her drop box preparations back in September by taking advantage of items that were on sale and running her food dehydrator night and day. They contained Lipton Dinners (removed from the package and resealed in the hikers friend - the ziplock bag!) breakfast foods and snacks, dehydrated chicken and turkey, vegetables and fruit which Mel had dried herself. Personal items such as travel size toiletries, socks, underwear, film, batteries, vitamins, aspirin and Ibuprofen were bought before hand to save money and were included in her boxes. Not all thru-hikers utilize maildrops but prior planning helped Mel's budget tremendously.

Our first camp was Hawk Mountain shelter and we had hiked eight miles to get there. Although the trail was wide and easy going, those first miles were celebrated with as much joy as our first 20 mile day would be later on in our journey, and we were happy to be there. Mel pitched her tent as the shelter was small and short on space, and Lindi unrolled her sleeping bag in the shelter. After dinner we would settle down and enjoy our first night on the trail as thru-hikers.

Most shelters on the trail have trail registers, an ordinary ruled college notebook in which hikers can record their name, a message for a partner or friend behind, or a line from a song, and it's usually signed not by one's real name but by a trail name. This is either given to you by other hikers or it's one that you have come up with yourself. Mel signed her first entry by her trail name Midnite given to her on a previous hike by her brother-in-law Terry, and Lindi became known as Out of Africa. Lindi was known as Red Apple at first because of her red jacket and red pack cover but she really didn't like it. After Neels Gap where she had bought a new jacket and another pack cover it suddenly dawned on her to be called Out of Africa. Had she stayed Red Apple she wouldn't have had nearly as much fun - Out of Africa's trail name was a great way to strike up a conversation.

Hawk Mountain was also memorable not only because it was our first night on the trail, but because we met hikers that would eventually be part of our trail family and also set us off on our journey of friendship. Out of Africa, being a dog lover was thrilled when Rat and his dog Tyco arrived at the shelter and after a while set about to win Tyco's affection. She would be rewarded later by Tyco sleeping on her sleeping bag with her. We were later joined by two other international members of our family Kiwi from New Zealand and Nursey from Switzerland.

Blood Mountain sits at 4,400 feet and is the highest elevation in Georgia. We had planned to stay at Blood Mountain Shelter our third day out but the task of carrying water a mile up to the shelter, a cold wind that had persisted for two days and had brought with it fog and drizzle, and rumors of an amorous skunk with a limp, persuaded us to hike two more miles to Neels Gap and a hostel. Although tired, we were proud of ourselves for hiking our biggest day so far, 14.6 miles, and looked forward to a warm shower. However, when we arrived at the hostel in the early evening, we found "no room in the inn" and the adjacent store about to close. We had forgotten it was Easter Sunday and had not anticipated that the hostel would be full. We were looking forlorn when a trail angel appeared in the form of a young man. He dusted us with our first piece of trail magic by offering to drive us the 3 miles to Goose Creek Cabins. When we had checked in the manager told us that two former thru-hikers had prepared a turkey dinner with all the trimmings for other thru-hikers. They wanted to pay back the trail magic they had received the previous year by hosting this dinner. We looked at each other with big eyes and happy grins as this was our second piece of trail magic and we gave thanks for these trail angels.

The next few days would put our determination to the test. After Out of Africa purchased rain gear and long johns at Neels Gap it began to snow and would continue to snow all day as we made our way to Whitley Gap shelter. Visibility was at a minimum and Out of Africa made a brief wrong turn when the white blazes were lost in the snow and fog. It was difficult to push ourselves to continue to hike without a break, but we were cold and wet and anxious to cover the eight miles to the shelter. We were greeted at the shelter by Zenwalker, Sissyphus the Happy and Jabberwaky huddled in their sleeping bags to stay warm. Social hour was brief that night.

Zenwalker was Canadian. He was a tall, slim young man in his middle twenties, with fair shoulder length hair worn in a pony tail. He had a very distinctive walk, and we learned to recognize him from a distance by his swinging two-poled gait. He would cover the miles easily and in one shelter he wrote, "Fifteen miles before lunch, Mmm, think I'll do a few more." He had the happiest smile and there was nothing selfish or mean in his character. He had teamed up earlier with Sissyphus the Happy, a blond, handsome hiker from Boston who possessed an awesome intellect. Jabberwaky had long black hair and always wore a three cornered jesters hat that was a gift from his wife before he started the trail. His disposition was always cheerful and optimistic.

The next morning was the coldest morning yet which shouldn't have come as a surprise as a skunk tried numerous times to make it into the warmth of Midnite's tent. A frozen tent zipper and frozen water bags made breaking camp unpleasant, and once again our fingers were soon numbed with the cold. We struggled with the valves on our stoves before we could gratefully wrap our hands around mugs of hot chocolate.

It soon became evident that hiking the A.T. was 95% mental and 5% physical. It was difficult to awake snug and warm in our sleeping bags knowing that as soon as we exited our cocoons the goal for the day would be to keep moving to stay warm. It also meant few breaks for us and how easy it would have been to roll over and go back to sleep, but our goal was to walk and walk we did.

We were more than ready for some sunshine and it came along just in time to ascend Tray Mountain. The sunshine would have been enough of a blessing for one day, but when we arrived at Tray Mountain Shelter we were greeted by Yogi who had been honing her "Yogiing" skills on some day hikers and was successful in acquiring some delicious goodies from them. Our appetizers for the evening's Lipton dinner were baby carrots, Pringles, fruit, and best of all, a funnel cake similar to the ones from a carnival. We were in thru-hiker heaven.

One of the reasons we wanted to thru-hike the Appalachian Trail was to meet people both on and off the trail in small town America. The Blueberry Patch in Hiawassee, Georgia was not a planned town visit, but we were glad that we didn't pass it by. Gary and Linnie Poteat welcomed us as one of their own to their hostel by providing a hot shower, doing our laundry and serving us a wonderful meal in their home.

April 12th marked the day we completed one state and our spirits were high as we stepped into North Carolina. One state down, 13 to go. Our joy was short lived as we climbed out of Bly Gap to Sharp Top. It was one of those climbs that seemed to go on forever and the highs and lows of the day had worn us out by the time we reached Muskrat Creek Shelter only to find it already full. We had already heard, through the trail telegraph, of the Kitchen Crew and this would be our first meeting with them. At the time we met them there were six hiking together and they carried everything except the kitchen sink, which they had sent back! Out of Africa enjoyed being at the shelters with them because Tigger always shared his imported coffee. He had brought along a real coffee grinder and he sat grinding his coffee beans like Kevin Costner in "Dances with Wolves."

We had read of the ascent up Albert Mountain and today was the day we would find out if it was as tough as the handbook said it was. It was a 1,000 foot hand over hand scramble over rocks in 2/10 of a mile and up until then we hadn't faced anything like it. Eventually, we stood at the top, slightly battered but elated, gazing at the magnificent view

Every dream of your heart is within reach if you believe in yourself

the climb afforded us. We felt as if we had just climbed Mt. Everest. We wondered how Tyco would manage but we neednot have worried about super dog. We had been there a little over ten minutes when Rat and Tyco appeared. Tyco, as usual, ambled up to us, his doggy packs swinging on his broad back and his tongue lolling out of his grinning face.

We felt we were beginning to hit our stride, physically and mentally. We knew before we started the trail that we wanted a partner to share the trail with, and were in awe of the solo hikers, especially females, who could not draw strength from a partner on those all too frequent difficult days. This was most evident after the Wayah Bald experience on April 15th.

The 11 miles into Fontana Dam, North Carolina would start out in the rain, but we barely noticed. We were headed for our first non-hiking day and Midnite's first maildrop which was being hand delivered by her parents. Our feet had wings as we approached the completion of our first goal but we did manage to take time to appreciate the wildflowers that were out in abundance. The rain had let up for awhile and we figured it was safe to take off our rain gear, but as we came to the road that would take us the two miles to Fontana Village, the clouds opened up and we were soaked in minutes. It had been seven days since our last shower, the longest period of time for both of us.

Fontana Village was more like a thru-hiker village. Hikers gathered around the Post Office sharing their treats sent from home in their maildrops and greeting other hikers as they came gratefully out of the rain onto the long porch. Even though Midnite's parents hadn't arrived from Ohio yet, we still felt as if we were meeting family. Fontana Dam would be the start of a trail tradition for Out of Africa and me for it was here I introduced her to Little Debbie Oatmeal Creme Pies. I had said that when we made it to Fontana all I wanted was a Mountain Dew and a Little Debbie and Out of Africa was more than happy to join me once we found them in the general store. From here to Katahdin this would become our ritual when our hiking boots hit town.

It was a joyous reunion for Out of Africa and me as we met my parents. I felt quite proud to have made it to Fontana Dam and we were both looking forward to some creature comforts. Nothing feels as good as that first shower and the home cooking I had been dreaming of for two weeks came tumbling out of the van when Mom and Dad opened the doors. During the months of planning my thru-hike with Out of Africa, Fontana Dam continually appeared in my mind, and quickly became my first goal. I honestly wondered during those months of preparation if I would reach that goal. Mt. Katahdin rarely entered my mind. My pride of making it to Fontana Dam was more than hiking 161 miles. Four years prior to our hike I was hospitalized and treated for Anorexia Nervosa, and battled my way back from weighing 74 pounds to 120 pounds. My friends told me even at 120 pounds there is no way I could carry 45 pounds and hike 2,159 miles. I told them: "It's not what you've got, but what you do with it."

CHAPTER 2

THE GREAT SMOKY MOUNTAINS, APRIL 21,1996

It seemed as if I had dreamed about the Smoky Mountains all my life and now I stood on the threshold. As as child I had daydreamed over photographs and said the name over and over to myself. A dream had come true, and now as I gazed over ridge upon ridge of blue mountains I had to keep saying to myself, "Out of Africa, you are truly here."

Out of Africa had picked up a tent in Fontana Dam and we entered the Smoky Mountains with seven days of food in our packs. This would be the last time that we would carry that much food with us and thereafter we vowed to keep things as light as possible. Our packs never exceeded 45 pounds and what we didn't have in them then, we figured we didn't need. We had been told time and time again, "The first three days are the hardest, after that it's just walking the ridges." The speaker would motion a straight line with his hand and we would look at each other with a silent, "Yeah right, BUT FIRST WE HAVE TO GET UP THERE!"

The "Get Up There" would be a long day out of Fontana Dam. After lunch we met Sluggo, a hiker from California who would join the growing number of our trail family and our paths would cross often between here and Katahdin. He was easily recognized by the fold up aluminium chair that he carried strapped to the back of his pack. We also met our first south-bound thru-hiker who had left Katahdin in August and we looked at him in awe, as he was about to complete his hike and we were just beginning.

We both had a different outlook on the possibility of encountering bears in the Smokies. Midnite had encountered bears before in the Shenandoahs and found them more wary of humans than the bears in the Smokies, and she would be happy not to see any sign of them. Out of Africa, on the other hand, couldn't wait to set her sights on one, but although other hikers spotted bears, we never saw any in the Smokies. In the 1800's wild boars had been imported from Europe for hunting. They had thrived and now roamed freely and although we saw plenty of evidence of where they had rooted near the trail, we were secretly glad that we didn't see any face to tusk.

Most shelters on the trail are three sided with an open entrance in the front. In the Smokies the front is enclosed by a chain link fence and gate to keep bears out. Mollies Ridge shelter was the first time that we had encountered such a bear fence. Even though the shelters were crowded the sense of protection we felt was worth the inconvenience. It was a beautiful setting for the hut, being in a meadow strewn with wildflowers and widely spaced trees that gave a feeling of space and light. We liked to think that we were hiking through the wilderness and it was always a surprise when we would see a glimpse of civilization. It was a shock to see the lights of Gatlinburg, Tennessee that had not been visible to us during the day.

Shelter life soon became routine. 1. Grab a space in the shelter. 2. Find the water source and filter water. 3. Remove boots. 4. Eat dinner. 5. Discuss the day's hike and discuss tomorrow's hike. 6. Prepare for bed. At least once (and usually more than once) the topic of conversation in the shelters would turn to food. Either the lack of it in our packs or what we were craving but would have to wait until our next town visit to satisfy. At Cosby Knob Shelter I would go to sleep that night with my appetite satisfied by a thru-hiker angel. Little Engine had hiked from town to the shelter and brought with her the ingredients for making S'mores. What a treat as Out of Africa and I snuggled in our sleeping bags and ate graham crackers with melted marshmallows and chocolate bars smooshed between them.

We were getting a taste of the changeable weather in the Smokies. One day sunny and warm, the next rainy and cold. On April 23rd we set out in the latter to climb Clingman's Dome. At 6,643 feet it is the highest point on the A.T. but it really didn't matter how nice the views were, we were fogged in. The descent from Clingman's Dome was in a river as the rains had flooded the trail. In our mudcaked boots we splashed and slipped our way down to our destination, Mt. Collins Shelter. Our spirits soared when the blue-blazed side trail to the shelter came into view, but would plummet when we realized it was another 1/2 mile to get out of the rain. We knew we were close to the shelter when we smelled wood smoke and couldn't wait to warm ourselves in front of a fire. However, we would have to wait our turn as the crowded shelter was overflowing with wet and cold thru-hikers. It was always difficult to force ourselves to go back outside in bad weather and filter as we did on this day and the water source was never close when the weather was nasty. It was an obstacle course trying to maneuver in the small shelter with wet clothes, gear and food bags hanging from every available nail. You couldn't walk without running into something or someone. We quickly learned to make the most of such a situation, and soon everyone was singing country songs while we all prepared our evening meals. We were all very warm while we slept, but then who wouldn't be with so many people in such a small area. The next morning, Chance, who was hiking with his wife Sassy, informed us that he was entertained during the night by watching the mice jump from one food bag to another. We all went to great lengths to hang our food bags from a string that had an empty can of some type suspended from the bottom of the string. The mice could run down the string and sit on top of the can, but were unable to get over the can, thus our food bags were mouse proof. But these mice were quite intelligent and where there's a will, there's a way when you're a hungry mouse with at least 16 food bags dangling in front of you.

It was in the Smokies, too, that we first thought of "scoring the triple." The perfect combination for a great shelter. The first was a spring - no need to filter water, the second was a privy - it eliminated the need to go digging in the woods, and the third a picnic table - it made cooking much easier and was good for socializing. It was hard to find a shelter with all three, but we were living in luxury when we did.

We left the Smokies behind, and in a rainstorm hiked down to Mountain Moma's Kuntry Store to meet Mimi and Jenny, two friends of Midnite's from Ohio who would hike two days with us. Sassy and Chance also hiked with us for a few days until they decided to push on to Browns Gap for the annual fish fry supplied by trail maintainers for thru-hikers. We opted to stay at Groundhog Creek Shelter and fore-go the crowds. As we were relaxing around a campfire, a southbound section hiker appeared and after introductions had been made she presented us with four oranges, gifts from Sassy and Chance. How sweet and refreshing they were and we savored every bite.

The next morning we stopped briefly at Browns Gap and introduced our taste buds for the second day in a row to more fruit before we hiked on. Tennessee has an abundance of bald mountains the origins of which are controversial but are basically mountains that are - well - bald! It was a relatively easy climb up Max Patch Bald and I kept expecting Julie Andrews to walk over the top singing "The Hills Are Alive with the Sound of Music." However, this would not have thrilled Out of Africa as this is her least favorite movie of all time. My rendition of the songs from that movie would motivate her over many mountains during our journey. We were instead met with a very strong wind which made walking on the top almost impossible.

We were about to reach another goal as we hiked into Hot Springs, North Carolina, a true Trail town according to The Thru-Hiker's Handbook, one of our "bibles" on the trail. The white blazes had brought us 250 miles from Springer Mountain. Out of Africa had been looking forward to staying at the Inn at Hot Springs for quite a few miles, a comforting promise we had made to ourselves. We met up again with Sassy and Chance and hiked into town with them. Without the full cover of leaves, it was unbearably hot. Sassy and Chance decided to go on to the Inn while we opted to stay one night at the Jesuit Hostel and the next night at the Inn.

While we were sitting around on the grass after our evening meal, we saw a group of hikers talking to a man in sweats, who we thought at first was a member of the hostel. We soon found out that he was Dan 'Wingfoot' Bruce, the author of The Thru-Hikers Handbook, and it was his custom to drop in to talk to thru-hikers.

The next morning we were up early to be sure to get a room at the Inn. Out of Africa was enchanted with the vast number of wooden homes in America and stopped frequently to admire them. The Inn was a Victorian two story white frame house, crammed with books, musical instruments and quilts. It was also reputed to have a ghost in room 3 - the room of Little Engine, but she told us, she never encountered it. The rooms were furnished with polished wooden furniture, deeply upholstered chairs and big comfortable beds. The bathrooms were big and airy with deep tubs and brass fixtures. It was sheer luxury. Far too nice for a dirty backpack. I had told myself prior to reaching Hot Springs that if I could locate a set of scales I would have to weigh myself. My biggest fear early in the hike was that I would start to lose weight and have to get off the trail. It was difficult for me to regain weight once I was in recovery from my eating disorder and every day I prayed that I had not lost any weight. Most thru-hikers need to consume 5,000-6,000 calories a day to maintain the strength needed to thru-hike and I would have to eat something every hour or so to try and satisfy my insatiable appetite. There would be days I would comment to Out of Africa, "I could sit down and eat EVERYTHING in my food bags." I was able to phone my mom and dad and report good news and bad news. The bad news was that I had lost weight, but the good news was that it was only one pound. I felt quite confident that if after 24 days I had lost only one pound I could maintain my weight. It was great to see Zenwalker again at The Inn, but he was struggling with the will to continue on the trail and would subsequently take a week off to sort things out. This was to be the last we would see Zenwalker for quite some time.

We had heard about a cabin that was lovingly tended by the caretaker and the entry in our handbook said "Last one out turn off the lights and please keep phone calls brief." Our curiosity made the shelter our destination for the day. Jerry Cabin shelter was set in a wide clearing, it had grass which was rare as up until then most of the shelters were set among rock and bare earth. On the wall inside someone had installed a telephone and a light socket. Needless to say neither were in working order, but we had a bit of fun when Midnite took the handset and ordered pizza to be delivered. We were still joking later when we announced, "Man that pizza is sure taking a long time!" One of the thru-hikers actually thought the phone was for real and was disappointed when we told her it wasn't.

The next day was a day for trail magic. Coming across a beautiful stream we spotted a large can of coleman fuel with a label attached which read, "Free to thru-hikers." Out of Africa was able to top off her fuel bottle thanks to the kindness of someone she would never meet and never be able to thank. She left a small flower on the can in thanks and hoped that her benefactor would understand. It was also a day of beautiful waterfalls and open meadows, and for the first time Out of Africa pitched her very own tent.

The next morning we once again had flying feet as we headed to Erwin, Tennessee and the completion of 337 miles, and another hand delivered maildrop by Midnite's parents, as well as a non-hiking day. This was also the day we met The Two Golden Kiwi's from New Zealand. They were a delightful couple in their late 60's and took great pleasure in video taping the many wildflowers in bloom. They were strong hikers and we had a great deal of admiration for them. I'm not sure if Out of Africa shared my sentiments, but I had written in my daily journal that, "I couldn't wait for morning so I could get up and walk again, it's like leaving on vacation every day."

You would think that thru-hiking the Appalachian Trail would be enough of an adventure, but I never knew what to expect when my family was involved. As Out of Africa and I descended to the Nolichucky River and Erwin, I could see my mom crossing the bridge towards the trail. Dad was waiting for us in the van instead of at the motel as we had arranged. She stopped and turned around to walk back to the van as she wasn't sure where the trail came out of the woods and in my excitement to stop her I shouted "Hey Lady." She recognized my voice and started towards us. I was never too dirty for a big hug. Once again the van was laden with food and our request to my mom as to what we were hungry for had been fulfilled. This week's craving was for toast and homemade jam and you can't have toast without a toaster! The next morning we soon found out that the smoke alarm worked in the motel as we toasted slice after slice of bread. Erwin was also the place where we sadly said our goodbyes to Sassy. She had struggled with a strained knee and had experienced dehydration a few days earlier. She decided that Erwin was as far as she could go. Chance would continue for some weeks without her.

It was always difficult to leave my family after a visit, but one day in town was enough for us. The noise of traffic and the fast-paced life of the real world soon had us on edge and once our feet were back on the trail we were glad to be there. We were enjoying the hike out of Erwin until the rain and the temperature began to fall. We had hoped to camp in a meadow for the night, but pitching a tent in the rain was our least favorite thing to do. Today was the day we developed, what would later be called, our "rain pace" and pushed 16 miles to Cherry Gap Shelter. Our rain pace was quite simple - put your head down and hike until you reach your destination. Rest stops are not an option, being warm and dry is. This was the first time I had been in such a downpour and commented to Out of Africa what an odd feeling it was to feel the water squish between my hips and the hipbelt on my pack. Sort of like hydroplaning with a pack on. Once I was in my rain pace I didn't notice the weight of my pack at all. I had only one thing on my mind - being dry.

After our mudfest of the previous day our legs felt like jelly as we set out for Roan High Knob Shelter. We could tell after our lunch break that we were quite tired and the endless climbs left us wondering if we could make it to a place to camp, let alone UP Roan High Bluff. We stopped for a break and decided that we would not push ourselves and continue only another half mile and stop for the evening. We both admitted to wanting to sit down and cry when we thought the climbs would never end, but pride is a hard to thing to swallow. It wouldn't take long for us to realize that over the next few months it was a great relief to let our emotions show rather than keep them in. That's why our friendship (and partnership) was becoming so strong. Being honest with each other on the days one or the other was struggling would help us over many mountains both physically and mentally.

It would turn out to be one of those days when everything went wrong. We were exhausted, and the trip to the water source, a barely running spring, left us totally frustrated. This was also the night that our water filters decided to malfunction, never-the-less we managed to collect enough to cook dinner and to fill our water bottles for the next day. My appetite had been relentless all day and that never made me a happy camper. Out of Africa was always very understanding when I became a little "testy" because on some days I couldn't seem to keep enough food in me. We were glad to crawl into our tents for the night and would awake the next morning to the most beautiful sunrise which helped ease the memories of the day before.

The shelters along the A.T. are usually constructed in the same manner, but Overmountain Shelter was an exception. A renovated barn with sleeping loft and an outstanding view of the valley below was a great place for lunch before heading up Hump Mountain. They were the most spectacular balds to date and Midnite was still looking for Julie Andrews to appear. The final bald gave us a taste of what ridge walking in the White Mountains of New Hampshire would be like - according to Iceman, a fellow thru-hiker. What a glorious feeling to walk effortlessly for a mile and have spectacular views all around.

We had heard rumors that Laurel Fork was not a particularly friendly area to hike through with its close proximity to a town. We were experiencing another one of those difficult days due to the warming temperatures and roller coaster terrain, and we should have been concerned when we saw a large sign hanging from a tree limb. In big red letters it read, "Beware of Shotgun." We were too tired to really worry about whose shotgun we should beware of and continued on to a beautiful gorge filled with rhododendron and pitched our tents. This would be the only warning of this type we would see on our journey. We were always amazed at how quickly our bodies would rebound after a good night's rest and some nutritious food.

The next morning I would experience my first injury and would rely on Out of Africa to help me, once I learned to swallow my pride. It was a very small stream with one slippery rock that sent my feet flying out from under me and my pack twisted my upper body in a direction it didn't care to go. After flailing in the water like a turtle on its back, my partner helped me to my feet and my immediate

What you get by reaching your destination is not nearly as important as what you will become by reaching your destination

thought was that I had cracked some ribs. As we ascended a hill I felt sure I had as it was painful to breathe. Luckily it didn't hurt to carry my pack, only to lift it on and off. Out of Africa was always there to lend a hand so I figured I would handle the pain until we got to a town and if it still hurt I would have it examined. The pain would persist for a week or so but eventually left me, only to reoccur in my mind when I crossed streams.

We were enjoying a beautiful, sunny day as we hiked into Laurel Gorge. The rhododendron was blooming at its peak and the pink flowers contrasted sharply with the gray of the gorge walls. We were looking forward to seeing Laurel Falls which was rumored to be spectacular. We were no more than a half mile away from the falls when it began to sprinkle so we quickly covered our packs and continued towards the roar of the falls. Before they came into view thunder rumbled and it began to pour. Our rain pace kicked in as Out of Africa was a little nervous about carrying her aluminum hiking stick with lightning crashing all around. We completely missed seeing the falls as our attention was directed to following the trail that hugged the river and wound over rocks and boulders. Had it not been storming we would have been much more cautious crossing the rocks, but once again our thoughts were of keeping us and our belongings as dry as possible so we heaved our bodies over them, and slid on the seat of our shorts down them as fast as we could to get to the shelter a half mile away. We were not quick enough and we arrived at Laurel Fork Shelter once again drenched.

We were out early the next morning to cover the seven miles to Hampton, Tennessee and Braemer Castle Hostel to dry out and re-supply. Sutton Brown, the owner of the hostel was one of those people who went the extra mile for thru-hikers. He is also the owner of Brown's Grocery, the only grocery store in town, but it is closed for business on Sundays which just happened to be the day we arrived. On arrival at the hostel, he informed us that he would let everyone into the store later that day for us to do our shopping. What a treat to have an entire grocery store all to ourselves. It would have been an even bigger treat to buy anything we wanted, but even though it was still early in our journey we had already formed a routine in what we would buy when we re-supplied. We could have walked down the aisles with our eyes closed. Pop Tarts and oatmeal for breakfast (the cream variety was our favorite) and we ate it cold since it was too much trouble to light our stoves in the morning. Lunch was equally as exciting, bagels (unless we couldn't find them, then it was English Muffins), honey or cream cheese would "garnish" them, dried fruit that Midnite dehydrated and had sent in her maildrops, fig newtons and pretzels. The piece-de-resistance was our evening meal. I was afraid Out of Africa would start growing "eyes" as she ate instant mashed potatoes EVERY NIGHT. Mind you she would really spice them up by adding butter buds or Parmesan cheese, but EVERY NIGHT. I didn't fare much better. It was either Lipton rice, or Lipton pasta and I added my dehydrated meat and vegetables. It was amazing what sounded so good when I was preparing my maildrops soon sounded as good as alfalfa sprouts. The "grazing" during the day consisted of granola bars which soon became lodged in my throat and were difficult to swallow, cheese and crackers, and gorp (Good Old Peanuts and Raisins). Mine consisted of peanuts, raisins and a *few* M & M's and Out of Africa's gorp consisted of M & M's ONLY. She, at one point, came out of town with a 2 lb. bag. She also enjoyed her bedtime snack of a dark Milky Way bar and would invert the wrapper and lick every bit off - we were never accused of wasting food. My bedtime snacks were not quite that exciting as chocolate did nothing for me except give me a sugar high. No wonder we craved Mountain Dew and Little Debbie's when we hit town.

Almost all of the hostels we stayed at had what were called "Hiker Boxes." These boxes contained various staples that hikers were either tired of eating, or things they didn't feel like carrying anymore. The items were free for anyone who thought they weren't tired of eating it, or felt like adding weight to their pack. You never knew what you might find in them, but mostly we found powdered milk, oatmeal (usually the regular flavor), and various Lipton dinners. We generally didn't need anything, but it was entertaining just to look through them.

Rarely did we stay in a town that didn't have a laundromat, but this was the case in Hampton. We always looked forward to washing our clothes when we were in town although we're not sure why. In a matter of days they would only get dirty again, but we did try to maintain some sense of cleanliness. Seeing that our only recourse was to wash them by hand we pitched them into the bathtub and watched as the water turned a very disgusting brown. Never have we seen so much dirt come out of clothes, but we figured they had to be better than when we walked into town.

It was at this point of our journey I began to notice the initial thrill of the hike beginning to fade. Out of Africa was experiencing these same feelings, but with my ribs continuing to hurt from my fall, my emotions were a bit more heightened. I was realizing that it was only mid-May and that from now until September (or possibly October) all I would do every day, day in and day out, would be hike, eat and sleep. It was quite a reality check for me and I would go through a roller coaster state of mind the next few days, but tried to keep in mind our goals and how hard I had worked to get this far. As we left Hampton we met Elf, who was attempting his second thru-hike and would give me a great deal of encouragement as well as inspiration. When we found the going especially tough we would draw on each other for that inspiration and encouragement. Navigating over a tricky stream, crossing or climbing over hazardous rocks, we would ask each other "How did Grandma Gatewood and Bill Irwin (who was blind) and his seeing eye dog Orient do this?" It was difficult for us at times and because we were younger than Grandma Gatewood by quite a few years, and unlike Bill Irwin, we had two good eyes, we would feel rather ashamed of ourselves for whining.

Our hike to Abingdon Gap Shelter started out uneventful but soon changed when two thru-hikers told us of an escaped convict who was on the loose. They had been stopped from continuing on the trail at a road crossing by the police the night before and told that the convict was within a seven mile radius of the trail. We were, of course, uneasy with this news and could hear helicopters from time to time which added to our anxiety. We were 21 miles from Damascus and thought if we would be alone at the shelter we would try to push on the extra miles. We were alert for unusual sounds and conscious of anything out of the ordinary. The shelter was empty when we arrived but we felt sure that Elf would stay there since we camped with him the night before and he did arrive shortly after we did. It was a restless night of sleep, but I must have slept at some point for when I awoke in the morning I found that Out of Africa had moved our packs into the shelter from the rain during the night.

CHAPTER 3

DAMASCUS, MAY 15, 1996

We had heard about Damascus and Trail Days from almost everyone we met. We arrived on Wednesday, in a rainstorm, after hiking the 10.3 miles in the record time of four hours. We paused briefly at the Tennessee/Virginia State line for our photographs. Posing in rain gear and covered packs, our faces peering out from under our sodden rain hoods, we managed to muster solemn smiles. After all, we were entering Virginia, our fourth and longest state, and we had covered 450 miles so far.

Damascus is known as the friendliest town on the trail and everyone wants to stay at "The Place" - a hostel run by the Methodist Church - a two-story structure that was already full of hikers who called greetings to us as we entered the hostel. We were soaked through from the rain but our mood was high, we had reached Damascus, a town rich in trail tradition. We had been talking for days about town food and couldn't wait to get to Quincy's so that Out of Africa could sample her first calzone. The menu was overwhelming with its many choices and EVERYTHING sounded good to us. After much deliberation, we finally decided on "starting off" with a salad, followed by a dinner plate size calzone oozing with cheese (which we shared) and topped it all off with a Philly Chicken sandwich piled high with peppers, onions and mushrooms. As our feast was set before us our friend Sluggo entered the restaurant and jokingly remarked that there was no way we could eat ALL of that. We of course proved him wrong!

We were glad to see Jabberwaky whom we hadn't seen for quite some time, but saddened to learn that he would be leaving the trail. He was enjoying his hike but missed his wife terribly. Out of Africa and I were also experiencing the homesick blues which I wasn't prepared for. When I was on the trail that's where I wanted to be, but it seemed that lately when we were in town and I called home, home is where I wanted to be. These feelings would be with me off and on for the remainder of the trip.

We decided to stay only one night in Damascus and skip the festivities of Trail Days. Thousands of people gather in town for three days of activities such as a pizza-eating contest, backpacker's parade, chili cook-off and a hiker's talent show. Both of us preferred the quiet of the trail rather than being part of such a large crowd.

White Top Mountain loomed large in our minds. We had heard reports on how difficult it could be in bad weather, and although the day started out overcast with a light mist, it quickly became worse. The hiking itself was easy enough and enjoyable, but by the time we reached Buzzard Rocks the mist was swirling thick and visibility was down to two feet. The white blazes were lost in the mist and we had to stop and wait until the 30-40 m.p.h. wind cleared a patch away before we could continue. One minute Midnite was visable, and the next she would be swallowed up in the mist. We could see nothing but what lay directly in front of us but as the mist rolled away, rocks and low lying plants suddenly became visible. The mist was so heavy that our hair and clothes were soon dripping with moisture and it was impossible for Midnite to see through her glasses, and removing them only made matters worse trying to see the blazes. It was a relief when we finally staggered down from White Top and into the relatively clear woods. We stopped and Midnite pulled her cigarettes from her pack. A light smoker, she put one in her mouth and drew deeply, blowing out a cloud of smoke she as said, "I might just sit here and smoke the whole pack!"

After a lunch eaten in the damp woods, we carried on to Mount Rogers. We had glimpses of open meadows but then the sun would go in again and the clouds would obscure the views. We were lucky that by the time we reached Mount Rogers, the sun had come out, the clouds had rolled away and we sat sunning ourselves on a rock before continuing to Thomas Knob Shelter. It was unbelievable how the weather could change so dramatically in so short a time and it was another lesson on how changeable the mountains can be. By the time we reached the shelter the skies were blue and we sat contentedly by the spring filtering water in the sun and talking. We climbed back up to the shelter and enjoyed a Coke we found, left for thru-hikers by a group of school children. We had emptied our packs and laid everything out in the sun to dry. Some weekend hikers came by and looked around, "Been here some time?" they asked. It probably looked as if we had taken up residence with our gear and damp clothes hanging from every available branch and bush.

The next day we set out for Grayson Highlands State Park and the wild ponies. The grasslands of the park have been likened to those of Montana with magnificent rock out croppings and the "big sky" reminded Midnite of her trip to Montana a few years earlier. That morning we had watched from our sleeping bags as the mist rolled across the shelter entrance, but by the time we were ready to hike, it had begun to disapate and we hoped for a clear day. Although we saw several tents of other hikers we had the Highlands to ourselves. The weather was sunny but not hot and it was a good day to hike. We could see for miles across the open spaces and it was a pleasant change from the woods. We were just bemoaning the fact that we hadn't seen any ponies when a small herd of six or seven strolled over a small rise and when Midnite saw that some mares had foals with them she hastily got her camera from her hip pouch. After that we saw quite a few small herds and were amazed that they could find enough to eat on the stubby vegetation.

I was very fortunate to have such a wonderful support team in my family and it didn't take them long to "adopt" Out of Africa. My father would comment that he was going to have to change his Will. My parents would become hiker central for me by adding to or taking things out of my drop boxes before mailing them, and visiting us in towns along the trail. They also provided endless love and support by mail and when I would phone home. May 19th brought us to Troutdale, Virginia, and another visit from my number one fans. As Out of Africa and I approached the road to town we were taking bets as to whether or not they would be there yet, when to our surprise my mom walked from behind a tree, camera aimed at us and exclaimed "What took you so long?"

We were both in need of a day off as the miles were beginning to take its toll on our knees. We also felt that we needed a mental break from our packs, but still wanted to cover some miles, so we decided a day of slackpacking was in order. What better place to arrange it but at The Fox Hill Inn at Troutdale.. David, the owner of the Inn, was more than accommodating as he dropped us off in the morning (minus our packs) and picked us up 23 miles later and drove us back to the Inn. It was a great feeling to be out from under our packs for a day and we felt as if we were literally flying without the weight of them. We met up with several members of our hiker family that day and it would also be the last time we saw Chance. We would later learn that he had left the trail to join Sassy at home, his desire to finish the trail left when she did in Erwin. We would spend another glorious night at the Inn before resuming our routine of hiking.

A curious incident happened at Knot Maul Branch shelter and I suppose somewhere someone is laughing at the trick they played on us. The shelter sits beside the trail and behind it on a small hill sits the privy. The privy had three sides and a good sized gap was left about head height between the roof and the walls. On one of the walls someone had left a boot. Because the trail passed right by the shelter it was easy to see who came by and who stopped. That night there was Midnite and myself, Elf, and Sluggo. Later on I again visited the privy and found that the boot had gone. I mentioned the incident to Midnite who said, "Yes, she had seen the boot earlier and also noticed that it was gone." I was puzzled about this for a while and I studied the boots of the other hikers. All of them, with the exception of Midnite's boots were leather and when I asked if anyone had left a boot up by the privy I was met with bewildered looks and shaking heads. I was confused now, since there were only the five of us that night and no other hikers had come by, so - who took the boot? "Is there," I wrote in the register, "a lone uni-hiker out there hopping along?" It would be months later as we hiked up a small incline to a main road in New York state that we saw, balanced atop the aluminium crash barriers, a lone boot and beside it a rough cut hiking stick! We began to laugh and wondered if Elf, who was ahead of us, was playing tricks and if he had played games with us back in Virginia. We never did find out.

May 25th we stayed at Davis Campsite, overlooking the beautiful Burkes Garden, referred to locally as God's Thumbprint. The day seemed endless to me as I toiled up the trail. The sun was hot and reflected off the many rocks on the ridges. There was no shady leaf cover and my face was a bright red as I sweated up yet another climb. I passed a party of high school kids who passed on a verbal message from my partner ahead, "Not much further." Thank goodness I thought and plodded on. I found Midnite in a small parking area near a dirt road, "Close your eyes," she ordered. I did as I was told and felt her wrap something icy cold around my neck. Midnite excitedly showed me a small pile of ice cubes that someone had dumped from their cooler. She took her bandana and wrapped the ice in it before laying it around my hot and sweaty neck! The simple pleasure of finding unwanted ice was like finding a pearl in an oyster.

We hiked into Bland, Virginia to re-supply and to meet Midnite's brother-in-law Terry who would be joining us for a few days of hiking. Terry and Midnite had hiked quite a bit of the A.T. over the last few years and she was thrilled that he came to hike with us. The terrain our first day out of Bland was relatively flat and we cruised the 12.1 miles to Jenny Knob Shelter by lunchtime. Terry was feeling good and since it was early in the day, we decided to push on a few more miles and pitch our tents. It sounded like a good plan, but a re-route of the trail left us without a water source or level ground to sleep on, so off we went again. Our day ended 18 miles later at Trent's Grocery where there was an area for thru-hikers to tent. Terry did miles his first day out that a lot of thru-hikers never did.

We decided the next day that we would do short mileage after our 18 mile trek and we were glad of that decision. After a stop at Dismal Falls it began to rain, lightly at first, but then it poured. It seems there was never any moderation with the rain - all or nothing. We were at Wapiti Shelter by early afternoon and settled in for a needed rest. When it rained on the trail, those thru-hikers who preferred to tent would push to make it to a shelter as was the case on this night and Terry had his first taste of a crowded shelter. Even with everyone sleeping on their sides, we still had no room to move.

The rains would continue off and on over the next five days and we would suffer greatly from them. The endless days of wet boots and feet seemed to affect me more than Out of Africa. We departed Rice Field Shelter after I had spent a sleepless night due to my aching knee. This was beginning to be an every night occurrence and troubled me as to what was causing the pain. It was not raining when we left and I had put on my last pair of dry socks and liners, but the undergrowth was still wet from rain during the night and within the hour my feet were soaked. My mental state was at its lowest point since leaving Springer Mountain and I had written in my daily journal the night before: "Is the human body suppose to be able to stand up to this day in and day out? Is all the pain worth what we will gain by hiking to Maine?" Those words came back to me as I felt my socks become saturated with water and tears filled my eyes.

I tried to remain optimistic each night, that the sun would shine down on us the next day and I could dry my boots and socks. I drew great strength from the slips of paper that my mom would send in maildrops with inspirational sayings and Bible quotes. I would take one out nightly and share it with Out of Africa. Though it wasn't raining during the day and the sun would warm our bodies, the underbrush would still be wet from evening rains or dew. The raw places on the tops of my toes were joined by blisters underneath, and each step felt like walking on sandpaper. I would become angry at my pain because the skies were blue and we were hiking through beautiful farmland but I was unable to enjoy it due to my discomfort. At Laurel Creek Shelter on the 30th of May I would write, "When do I decide when I'm in too much pain to still be out here?" My knee at this point hurt up into my thigh and I wondered how much more I could take.

The following day I started out in dry boots and socks but this was little comfort after another sleepless night with

To be without justification is acceptable

my knee. Despite my fatigue I felt my mental attitude was improving and Out of Africa and I were chatting and enjoying a beautiful morning filled with sunshine. Before I realized it, we were in a pasture field with grass to our knees that was wet with dew. I stopped and cried out "All I want is one day of painless walking," and did not have the courage to take one more step. Once again, Out of Africa offered me her shoulder to cry on and gave me some encouraging words to motivate me to carry on. As I did so many times during our hike, I asked God to give me strength and if it was His will for me to continue this journey, I would.

The first day of June found us dreading the hand-over-foot descent of Dragon's Tooth. We expected it to be difficult and were not disappointed. It was only a half mile descent, but seemed like ten as we slid down sheer rock faces. We would no sooner master one and another would appear that would leave us shaking our heads and our knees feeling like jelly by the time we were finished.

Our knees would not get any rest the next day as we made our way to McAfee Knob, one of the best photo opportunities on the trail. It was a moderate climb to get there and we were both anxious to see this anvil shaped rock reaching out into space. This was one of the most spectacular views we would have and the valley below was breathtaking. We stopped for an early lunch and were joined by two hawks who soared above our heads. It was difficult to leave this spot, but Tinker Cliffs awaited us. The trail followed the edge of these cliffs and we kept looking for "wild" goats that reportedly wandered up to hikers and sometimes licked the sweat off their legs. To our dismay we didn't see any and a fellow thru-hiker was equally dismayed as he wrote in the register at the next shelter "I want sweat licking goats damnit, I could do with a good licking."

Our destination on this day was Lamberts Meadow Shelter. Our handbook said that copperheads had been seen near the rocks of the fire pit and to exercise caution. We were hoping since we didn't see the goats maybe it wasn't our day to see wildlife and we wouldn't see any snakes either. We settled in for the evening and as we often did, read the trail register as we ate our dinner. There was an entry from Elf who had stayed the night before that said he was kept awake all night by rats in the shelter. We were quite used to mice by this time but hadn't yet encountered rats! We hoped we would be three for three today on the wildlife tally, since so far the copperheads had not shown themselves. Soon after dinner, Out of Africa was in the shelter and yelled that she had seen a rat poking its head through the floor of the shelter and that she could hear them "talking" as well. We figured we could place rocks over the cracks in the shelter floor and that would keep them at bay for the night. As fast as we would cover one hole, another head would peek at us through another. We knew that we wouldn't get any sleep and agreed that sleeping with mice was one thing, but rats was something else. We loaded up our gear and hiked another mile to a stream, made camp for the night, and had a peaceful night's rest.

We were anxious to get to Troutville, Virginia the next day as Midnite's parents were once again making the pilgrimage to meet us. We had read in the shelter register the night before that Zenwalker was getting off the trail in Troutville and we were hoping to see him in town. We were able to locate him at an adjacent motel and spent some time talking with him about his decision. He felt his heart wasn't in the trail anymore, but in Canada with his girlfriend. He had already spoken with her, as well as his family, and they had persuaded him to give it another try and not make a hasty decision. We were thrilled that he took their advice and went back out the next day.

Troutville is where we learned that two female hikers had been murdered. They were camped in the Shenandoah National Park in Virginia and their lives were taken while they slept. It was a senseless tragedy that would leave a dark cloud hanging over the trail for quite some time and affect most thru-hikers, male and female alike. We received a call from my sister Lesa in Ohio informing us of the brutal crime. My family, Out of Africa and myself would spend the next few hours trying to decide if we should go on. Understandably, my parents and the rest of my family were very upset and concerned for our safety. I felt torn in two. My head told me it would be safe as long as we stayed close to the shelters, and in order to do that we would have to hike big miles every day. My heart, on the other hand, did not want to put my family through the worry. My mom finally said to me "I can't let you go back out there" and all I could think of was all the pain and worry I had put them through over the last few years with my illness and here I was about to do it again. We would not be in the Shenandoahs for another two weeks and we finally agreed that we would see what those two weeks would bring and hopefully they would catch whoever had done this. It was with a very heavy heart that I left town the next day and my feet felt as if they had cement blocks on them.

The first day out of Troutville we met a hiker who we would truly call a friend. We first saw him at Wilson Creek shelter where we stopped for a break. He was sitting at the picnic table with some other hikers, and the expression on his face totally mislead us as to his personality. His expression clearly said, "Life sucks!" Buzz was 27, a 6' 4" giant who towered over most other hikers. He had thick brown hair and a golden beard. By the time we reached Harpers Ferry, WV, Buzz had lost an amazing 50lbs in weight!

We saw him later at Bobblets Gap Shelter. We stayed the night there along with Jackstraw, a thru-hiker, who had the most luxuriant strawberry blond hair and beard. By day he wore his hair tied back, covered by a bandana tied pirate style. That same day we celebrated our three month anniversary on the trail. Life on the trail was good. We had made many friends and we felt at home. I can't remember when the feeling of uneasiness in the woods left me. I just remember thinking one day as I walked along the trail how peaceful it was and how normal it felt to be there. Perhaps these feelings came from building up friendships and being able to walk into a shelter and feel at home with the people there. I always think of Midnite saying it was like coming home after a hard day at the office, and shouting out "Hi, honey I'm home."

On June 8th we crossed the James River. As we stood on the bridge looking down river I saw in my mind how the English ships must have looked all those centuries ago as they sailed up the wide beautiful river. How the people on board must have gazed in wonder, as I was doing now, at the thickly wooded hills. We walked on, eventually catching a lift to Wildwood Campground, four miles away. We rented a small camper and decided to have a relaxing day, that is after we had resupplied, done our laundry and had showers. I was delighted to find a stove in the camper and bought milk and tea and had my first real cup of hot tea since Troutville and I happily made myself five cups! British style with milk - no sugar or honey- ugh! Jackstraw and Buzz joined us at the campground but they had decided not to stay the night but to go on to the next shelter. They ate breakfast and lunch and were still there at 4:30 p.m.!

We would be hiking in the Shenandoahs in eight more days and my family was growing more concerned and expressed their uneasiness with each phone call home. While at Wildwood Campground my mom told me that she wanted Out of Africa and me off the trail as she was afraid for our safety. My emotions were raw as we tried to decide what to do. I could tell by my mother's voice how distraught she was, and the closer we came to the Shenandoahs the more uneasy we were becoming. I made phone call after phone call trying to come up with an alternative plan such as slackpacking through the area, or skipping it altogether and completing it after we climbed Katahdin. The first option I soon found would be costly as well as logistically difficult, and neither of us wanted to do the second. We kept coming back to the idea of someone to "babysit" us at the shelters each night and I decided to leave an entry in the next shelter register that we were looking for someone. This helped to ease my mother's mind and we would have one more town visit before the Shenandoahs and we both prayed we would find someone to stick with us and I could set my family's mind at ease. I was not at all happy with the entire situation. I felt we had been robbed of our freedom that we both had been enjoying up until this point and suddenly one of the "normal world's" problems was encroaching on our territory and our carefree existence was now threatened.

It was raining heavily the next day as we trudged up to Punchbowl shelter and while we ate our lunch we decided to call it a day. We were already soaked. The sky was a heavy slate gray with no sign of letting up. A few minutes later Buzz hurried in, sat cross legged while eating and gazed out of the shelter. He decided to have a nap while waiting for Jackstraw to catch up. When Jackstraw finally made it to the shelter he ate a quick lunch and announced his decision to carry on to the next shelter since he was already wet. We were glad when it was evident that Buzz had decided to stay. He sat reading through the register and when he came to our plea for a "babysitter." He told us, "I'd be glad to hike with you guys." We thanked him, but told him that we felt comfortable during the day but would feel better just to meet someone in the shelter at night. We felt this would help ease the minds of Midnite's family. We discussed with him our plans to slackpack out of Waynesboro the first day into the Shenandoahs. He nodded, studying his Data Book. "You can slackpack with us, if you like," we said. Buzz shook his head, his bangs hanging over his eyes. "No, I'll meet you at Blackrock shelter, but I'll carry my pack." So it was arranged, almost casually, that Buzz would meet us at the shelters in the Shenandoahs, still five days ahead. He would wait for us in Waynesboro, since he planned to be there two days before us, for tomorrow he was going to catch up with Jackstraw - as it turned out it would be a 25 mile day for him.

Later on that evening, a group of thru-hikers known as The Disciples arrived one at a time. They had met at Springer Mountain and decided to team up. There was Jeff and Greg, two ex-Army Rangers who had left the service only weeks before they started the trail. Jeff had a quick wit that held his audience spellbound while he told his funny stories. Greg was quieter, with shinning eyes full of wry amusement. Stephen had come from Australia to hike the trail, and held a PH.D in Mathematics, something we found out much later. Dave was the fourth member, quiet and unassuming, and he would have looked at home in a college lecture room.

The next morning we had our usual early morning rain. It was becoming routine for it to pour on us around 9:00 a.m. and then by afternoon the sun would make an appearance and the humidity would be unbearable. After a long 15 miles we arrived at Cow Camp Gap Shelter and attempted to dry things out. We were surprised to have the shelter all to ourselves and felt a little uncomfortable at the prospect of being alone given the recent circumstances. We really were not totally alone as there were a number of very friendly mice in the shelter. I remember thinking how cute they were as they scurried along the beams of the shelter and I commented to Out of Africa that they were by far the most social mice we had seen thus far. We always left the pockets on our packs open at night so the mice could run in and out instead of chewing their way into our packs to make sure we hadn't left any morsels of food. (Fat chance of us leaving food anywhere unconsumed.) Upon awaking the next morning I glanced up at my pack hanging from a peg on the shelter wall and caught a glimpse of a long tail disappearing into the top of it. There was no way I was going to carry any extra weight in my pack, although it was incredibly cute, with beady eyes gazing up at me. I gently lifted my pack down from the peg and carried it to the edge of the shelter and set my new friend free. Upon further examination of my pack I discovered my (now not so cute) friend had been busy during the night as I removed a pile of leaves it had gathered for its bed.

The Waynesboro Fire Department allowed hikers to pitch their tents on the small piece of lawn at the side of the fire house and we had originally thought about doing that, but when we got there we found the space taken by Buzz, the Disciples, Birdsong and Sunbeam. We gratefully took showers and went out to re-supply at the grocery. By the time we came back it was so hot that we decided to go to a motel, especially since Midnite's brother Stephen was joining us for the night. We were glad we did; while the others were at the cinema, a thunderstorm moved in and everyone was flooded out.

The next day was our slackpack day, and we planned to meet Buzz at Blackrock Hut, 20.1 miles away. We had been on the trail about ten minutes when we were joined by another "partner" for the day. Instead of two legs and a backpack, she had four legs and a tail. She was a beautiful hunting dog, sleek and alert. We tried a number of times to send her home and sometimes as she dashed off on a scent we breathed sighs of relief, thinking that she would now return home, wherever that was, but five minutes later we would hear her behind us again. She stopped when we did, took no food from us and was always eager to get going again. We named her Shan, because we had just entered the Shenandoah National Park and discussed how we would feed her on the way to Maine. She stayed with us the whole day, easily covering the twenty miles. We were worried by this time because we had no idea of how to get her back, but the couple who brought our packs to us said they would return her when they left and we waved a sad goodbye to our hiking partner.

We slung our heavy, re-supplied, packs on our backs and started off for Blackrock Hut. This was also a reunion of sorts since friends of Midnite's from the Buckeye Trail in Ohio were joining us for the evening before hiking out the next day and returning home. Herb and Susie had brought chocolate chip cookies and cherry crisp from Midnite's parents. Everyone had a fork and dug in eagerly. We were also introduced to Wildflower at Blackrock Hut. She was a lone hiker from Florida and in her late 40's. We admired her courage and determination to complete the trail. Wildflower carried a lightweight hammock with her and would string it up for an afternoon siesta.

We began to wonder about Buzz. It wasn't uncommon for him to hike until early evening but there was still no sign of him when darkness fell and since he had promised to be at the Hut we could only hope that he was safe and we tried not to worry. He was more than capable of taking care of himself, but our trail family received the same caring thoughts as our real families at home.

As usual we were up early in the morning and on the trail by 6:30 a.m. This seemed to us to be the best time of day to be on the trail, the woods were alive with birds and insects. We said goodbye to Herb and Susie and started off down the trail. Midnite came to an abrupt halt, just ahead of her on the trail were two romping bear cubs. We could hardly believe it when a third cub broke from the woods and joined the others. Midnite reached for her camera only to freeze as Mama bear lumbered out of the woods to our right, gave us a brief glance and followed her scampering cubs into the woods again. Our emotions were mixed with fear and excitement when we would see potentially dangerous wildlife. We both had a great respect for all of nature as we were "visitors" in their home and respected them as we wished to be respected by visitors in our own home. To come so close to such a powerful and magnificent animal as the black bear would raise the hair on the back of our necks one minute, and our hearts would melt the next as we watched the cubs rolling over themselves in play. We felt very fortunate at having seen such a lively family but thought it prudent to give them breathing room before we continued on our way. We saw a total of five bears while we were in the Shenandoahs. Out of Africa jokingly said that she could now go home as she had seen her bears!

The Shenandoahs were alive with wildlife. The deer seemed so tame and would watch us as we walked within a few feet of them but they would only allow us so close before taking off into the woods, It seemed that at every bend in the trail there were deer, squirrels, chipmunks and rabbits. Hard to believe that in such a tranquil place two innocent women had had their lives stolen from them. Every hiker we passed on the trail was a source of information for us on the latest developments in the search for the person(s) responsible for the murders. For the first time since leaving Springer Mountain we had a hunger for news. Our hearts were saddened with each response of "They still don't know anything."*

We were surprised and delighted when Buzz showed up at Pinefield Hut later that evening. He apologized for not being with us the previous night but explained that he had been delayed by the storm in Waynesboro and was half an hour away from the shelter and hiking in the dark when his head lamp blew out. It was 10:30 pm and it was too dark for him to go any further, so he threw down his sleeping bag and spent the night in the middle of the trail. We were touched by how hard he had tried to keep his promise to meet us at the shelters.

In June the rains came daily. Fortunately most days we were safely in the shelters and stayed dry but once or twice we were caught. The rain fell with such force that within minutes the trail was running water and we were so wet that when we took our boots off we were able to pour water out of them and wring our socks, shorts and t-shirts out. Buzz, being so tall, had no difficultly in hanging his food bags on the bear poles in the Shenandoahs, but he told us it took

*At the time of publication, these murders still had not been solved.

some hikers quite a few attempts before they were successful. The poles are metal, 20 feet in height with a cross beam at the top to loop the handle of the food bag over. The difficulty is in being able to maneuver the long pole with which you hoist the food bag up. Out of Africa received a lesson from Buzz and was successful on her first attempt, much to the dismay of the watching males!

Front Royal, Virginia marked the end of the Shenandoahs. We were sorry to leave them. We had enjoyed the rolling terrain and the easy, well maintained trails. To save money we shared a motel room with Buzz, and after some deliberation decided that we would go Mexican for dinner. It was heaven after the bland trail food and afterwards we treated Buzz to ice cream - a quart for him and a pint for each of us. We spent the rest of the evening eating ice cream and watching TV. The next day Midnite paid for her indulgence, and decided that spice and dairy had no place in her diet while on the trail. From Front Royal to Katahdin she was always careful and had no desire to repeat the battle of the intestines. How frustrating it was to dream of town food and know that upon arrival in town it would have to be eaten in moderation.

We had good times with Buzz and the Disciples. Buzz had many stories that could only happen to him. Not long after we first met him he told us about a girl he met in a restaurant in Catawba, Virginia. She was sitting with her mother in the adjacent booth and after a while came up to him and asked him if he was a thru-hiker. When he said he was she asked if she could take a photograph of him. He agreed and they went outside. Once outside she said that she would like to take his photograph on the trail and he agreed to go with her in her car. (The more harden among us are by this time giving knowing nods) Arriving at the trail they got out of the car and she thrust a stuffed toy into his arms. She told him it was a seal and it's name was Flat Sammy. He had to hold it so she could show her friends. It was never fully explained why he had to stand there holding her stuffed seal but Buzz didn't care. Nothing bothered Buzz.

Another time he joined us at Pass Mountain Hut in the Shenandoahs. He came in wet and said that he had done something he had never done before in a restaurant. The hut went silent as he confessed he had eaten off the leftover menu. What leftover menu we wondered. He explained that he had been sitting in the restaurant and noticed a boy of about 13 sitting with his family opposite him. The boy had ordered shrimp but didn't touch them, instead he ate his french fries and pushed the shrimp to the side of his plate. When the family left, Buzz got up casually and took the boy's plate and ate the shrimp. "I saw the waitress giving me dirty looks," he shrugged, "But I didn't care."

The time we spent in Front Royal with Buzz was probably the funniest. He had gone to the laundromat to do his laundry and as usual he didn't have any clothes to change into while his clothes were in the washer. He asked the assistant if there were any clothes that he could wear while he waited. She brought back the only only item of clothing in the place, a pair of girls stretch pink shorts! Buzz being Buzz didn't hesitate putting them on - there he sat in the laundry reading until his clothes were ready. "Not a pretty sight," he said later.

In Harpers Ferry, WV we stayed in a bed and breakfast across from the Appalachian Trail Conference. Allison, the kind owner, was doing Buzz's laundry and since Buzz only had the clothes he hiked in she had leant him a pink bathrobe. Allison was not a tall person and the robe came mid thigh on Buzz, but he nonchalantly ambled across the road and sat talking with some hikers who had just come in.

The view from the peak will justify the pain of the path

CHAPTER 4

HARPERS FERRY, WV, JUNE 26, 1996

We have made it to Harpers Ferry, West Virginia, the unofficial halfway point of the trail. Considered by many thru-hikers as the psychological halfway point, it is the home of the headquarters of the Appalachian Trail Conference. For weeks we had been dreaming of reaching this point. We were numbers 248 and 249 to pass through the conference center, a charming stone building on a quiet street. We posed outside for the official photograph with our usual town "props" - a Little Debbie Oatmeal Creme Pie and a Mountain Dew. The photographs are then put in a photo album with names and dates of arrival. The book is popular with thru-hikers as they can finally put a face to the names they have been reading in the trail registers for 994 miles. Harpers Ferry is steeped in history and it seems to cling to the shore of the Potomac River. Across the swirling brown water, the cliffs rise steep and stark. Now used for rapelling, the cliffs once hid soldiers who kept the residents of Harpers Ferry pinned down by rifle fire.

We checked into a bed and breakfast across the street from the conference and patiently waited for Midnite's family to arrive from Ohio. We had decided to take advantage of being in a town rich with history and take two days off from hiking and do some sightseeing with Midnite's family. The arrival of Midnite's sister Lesa, niece Ashley, nephew Adam, and her parents made Midnite realize how much she was missing her family and spending two days with them made it very difficult to return to the trail. We were feeling very optimistic and enthusiastic about reaching the official halfway point in Pennsylvania, 89 miles away, and as usual, Midnite's family encouraged us to continue to put one foot in front of the other, and take one mile and one day at a time. I told Out of Africa, as we left Harpers Ferry, that my father has always been supportive of me in all my endeavors. As he and I said our goodbyes, the look in his eyes and the words he spoke to me, "Just don't give up, You can do this," sent chills up my spine and was more than just support, it was passion for me to fullfill my dream. I would invision my father's face and draw on those words time and time again over the months ahead.

West Virginia was definitely our easiest state. The trail covers only 2.4 miles and it is along the C & O Canal towpath and is perfectly flat. The state of Maryland did not pose much of a problem either as we gazed down on the Shenandoah River from Weverton Cliffs. This is one of the most photographed places on the A.T. We thoroughly enjoyed the relatively easy 41 miles to complete two states in three days. We really felt as if we were making progress after spending almost six weeks hiking through the state of Virginia.

June 31st brought us to Pen Mar County Park, two-tenths of a mile from the Pennsylvania state line. We had our first battle with mosquitoes that morning as they swarmed around us continually and left me feeling less than motivated to continue hiking the rest of the day. Out of Africa and I stopped for an early lunch at the pavilion in the park and reluctantly shouldered our packs to move on. Suddenly, a group of young girls appeared and began the 20 questions that are so frequently asked of thru-hikers. "Where do you sleep? How far have you come? How much do your packs weigh? Have you seen any snakes?" and the inevitable, "Why are you doing it?" My answer of "pursuing my dream and experiencing living with nature for six months" provided the motivation I needed for the day and reminded me to live in the moment, and not worry about what happened yesterday, or what might happen tomorrow. So many times during our walk, someone or something would inspire me to think positively and I firmly believe that God was that someone and that He would also provide us with the something to keep us on track.

We were beginning to hike over the much talked about Pennsylvania rocks as we entered Pine Grove Furnace State Park, home of the official halfway point and the half-gallon club. The rumors of how difficult the trail would be in traversing the rocks were varied. "They really aren't too bad" one hiker would tell us, and the next would look wide-eyed and comment "They are horrible." Our handbook's comment on the rocks was: "The rock garden at the Bleu

Blaze Hostel is reportedly the nursery for those sharp little rocks you'll be going over on the footpath" only reinforced our lack of enthusiasm for this section of the trail. We were to meet Midnite's brother-in-law, Terry and nephew, Adam at the hostel in the park and they would be hiking with us for a couple of days, but first Out of Africa would try to become a member of the half-gallon club. It is a trail tradition that upon reaching the halfway point that you eat (or try to eat) a half-gallon of ice cream of your choice as fast as you can. If you succeed at this feat, you receive the ice cream free and are presented with a commemorative wooden spoon from the convenience store next to the hostel. Midnite would have nothing to do with this as she still had a clear image of her ordeal with town food in Front Royal, but Out of Africa was ready to give it a go. She did quite well eating about 3/4 of it and swore that had it been a hot day instead of cool and overcast, that she would have succeeded. Our friend, Oops, faired better and not only ate one half-gallon, but waited an hour and ate another becoming the first thru-hiker to do so. We would not see Oops for a couple of days but heard through the grapevine that he was alive and well and carrying 2 wooden spoons. The trail register at the store revealed the sad news that our dear friend Zenwalker was ending his hike. We would miss his smiling face on the trail, but applaud his decision to return to Canada to be with his girlfriend. The trail will always be there to finish for those who choose not to continue. It takes as much courage to end a hike prematurely than to push to carry on when your heart is not in it. Completing the trail is not as important as the fact that we pursued our dreams.

The 4th of July dawned clear and beautiful for our joyous walk to the halfway marker of the trail. At 6:15 a.m. we stood in front of the sign showing Springer Mountain 1,069 miles heading south, and Mt. Katahdin 1,069 heading north. (The actual mileage changes every year due to relocations of the trail) Up until this point we had not really allowed ourselves to think about reaching Katahdin, but now we both felt that if we could make it halfway, we could make it all the way. Our confidence level was very high as we took our first step on the second half of our journey. We had learned so much in these first 4 months about the trail and each other. We had helped each other in so many ways and our partnership had grown into a beautiful friendship. We would often laughingly act out the Chip and Dale cartoon- the two polite chipmunks who always insisted the other go first: "Before You, No, No, No, Before you, I Insist." Our decisions on the trail were not what was best for ourself, but best for us, and it seemed, at times, that we were one in the same. Our spirits were soaring and so were our feet as we covered 12 1/2 miles before lunch and arrived at Kennedy Shelter by early afternoon where we had planned to stop for the night. We decided to take a long break, cook an early dinner and hike another 3.9 miles into Boiling Springs to camp. It was such a glorious day and as we descended into Boiling Springs, the view of white farm houses and fields of wheat and corn was something straight out of a Norman Rockwell painting. Truly Americana!

A good water source was always a pleasant surprise after a long day and was always the first thing we would search out upon arrival at the shelter. Our handbook would sometimes give us a "sneak preview" of what to expect which was sometimes good and bad. We really scored a triple with Peters Mountain Shelter - a luxurious two story shelter, nice composting privy and a piped spring. The handbook entry for this shelter said, "The reason the spring is so cold, it's in Canada" was not wrong. It was a beautiful piped spring, but was at least a 1/2 mile DOWN and the cooling effect it had on us was short lived as we had to hike back UP. An entry in the register was a cartoon depicting the walk to the spring. It showed a backpacker rapelling down the side of a cliff following a sign marked "Spring."

It was at this point that the rocks were beginning to take their toll on our feet. During the day our soles felt as if they were one big stone bruise and ached with every step, and at night we would lie on our bags and feel them pulsate and twitch in pain. The rocks were unbelievable. In some parts of the trail they were large and we were able to hop from one rock to the next, and other sections were smaller pointed rocks that would roll our ankles, or we would stub our numb toes on them and wince in pain. Our feet were, simply put, a mess. Blisters on the tops, as well as the bottoms of our toes were eased with the help of duct tape. We would apply liquid 1st Skin to the raw places on our feet followed by a patch of 2nd Skin, topped with moleskin and all held in place by a piece of duct tape. Nothing else would stand up to the abuse we put our feet through. Duct tape had many uses in our pack. We would have to continue with trail conditions like this for the next 100 miles until we reached Delaware Water Gap and entered into New Jersey. The physical pain was not the only problem we were having. The rocks were also affecting us psychologically. With every step we were afraid of twisting our ankles which might force us off the trail and it became a real struggle to decide where to place each foot. There were times when I would stand and look left and right and not be able to make a decision as to which way to go and I cried out to Out of Africa one afternoon, "How can one state possibly have so many rocks." The indecisiveness left me mentally exhausted.

We were really looking forward to staying at the 501 Shelter as it was our first shelter that was completely enclosed and even came equipped with a skylight. We were joined that night by a diverse group of hikers: three male high school section hikers, our friend Buzz, and Captain Chucky and Heavy Breather, a father/son thru-hiking team. It was so refreshing to be able to interact with such a group that given the same circumstances in the "real world" might not lend to such a fun and carefree evening.

I was beginning to feel pressure, pressure that I put on myself, to cover miles and take less time off in town and those feelings were present as we left 501 Shelter. We were headed for Pine Grove, Pennsylvania to meet my parents and pick up another maildrop. Out of Africa also seemed less enthusiastic about town visits and we were beginning to talk more about reaching Katahdin and felt an unexplained sense of urgency to get there. Upon arriving at the motel where we were to meet my parents, we received a phone message for me to call home. My heart sank and I feared the worst as I dialed the number. My father had taken a fall and injured his hip that he had had replaced a few years ago. He was doing fine but they would not be able to join us for our day off. Needless to say I was disappointed as I always looked forward to seeing them and had it not been for the fact that we had to wait for my maildrop, we would have left immediately for the trail. The day dragged on forever as I waited for delivery of my box that had been sent by overnight mail. It was most urgent that I receive it as it contained my new boots to replace the 1,000+ mile pair that were currently on my feet. Its arrival sent us into our town mode of unpacking and repacking our packs for another departure and the realization that I would not see my parents again until we reached Maine made for my most unpleasant town visit.

The trail was always full of surprises and July 13th found us hiking in the aftermath of Hurricane Bertha. We had been hearing reports that our area would be hit with heavy rain and high winds, but that didn't stop us as we set out from Windsor Furnace Shelter in a slight drizzle. As usual, ten minutes on the trail found us in a downpour and our rain pace kicked in and pushed us the 10.6 miles to Eckville Shelter once again soaking wet from head to toe. This shelter was similar to 501 Shelter as it was fully enclosed but MUCH smaller and as we pushed open the door found it already full at 10:00 a.m. Captain Hook whom we hadn't seen since Hot Springs, NC introduced us to Morning Glory, Mud Puppy, Blister Sister, and Julie McCoy-Cruise Director, that is after they finished singing this rather strange song about petunias. We wanted to be out of our wet clothes and really didn't care to be taught the words to this camp song, but as so often happened, once we were warm and dry our spirits lightened and soon the sun was shining and we gathered outside at the picnic table for an encore performance of "petunia."

Lehigh Gap is a huge jumbled mountain of rocks, haphazardly thrown down by some huge upheaval. It's referred to as Dante's Inferno because on a hot day the heat radiated back from the rocks is as hot as an oven. Fortunately, the day we climbed was misty and so windy at the top, it filled our pack covers like sails. I always enjoyed rock climbing much more than Midnite. I found it exciting and challenging. It also passed the time much quicker than solid hiking, but on a steep upward gradient, Midnite would also leave me behind. Still, I remember "pulling a face" when I saw the mountain as we crossed the Lehigh River. "I hope we're not climbing up there," I called in disbelief to Midnite, but after crossing the road, we could see that the white blazes were leading straight up and as far as we could see, over the top. We often thought of the older thru-hikers, like the Golden Kiwi's and the Western Canada

Geese, and especially Wildflower. If we found it hard, it must have been tougher for them.

Our legs were extremely tired and our feet had been bothering us for days and did not have alot of miles in them for the day as we gazed up at the mountain of boulders that laid between us and a camping spot for the night. We stopped for a break and Midnite said a silent prayer for God's help to give us strength and patience to conquer yet another obstacle of granite and stone. Once again we relied on each other for moral support and an outstretched hand to heave our exhausted bodies up and over the rocks. Upon reaching the top we were quite proud of ourselves for accomplishing what seemed an impossible task and looked forward to an easy walk to the spring and pitching our tents for the night. We were unable to locate the water source and reluctantly pushed on to the next one listed in our guidebook only to be disappointed again by not being able to locate it. Our mental attitudes were quite low and we both decided a few creature comforts were needed and pushed on to a road crossing that would take us to Slatington, Pennsylvania. It was one of those rare occasions that we were unable to hitch a ride into town and with our heads hung low we began to walk, hoping to come to a phone so we could call for a shuttle to a motel. A 1/2 mile of road walking brought us to a sign announcing the Blue Mountain Ski Lodge and after asking a passing motorist if they were open and had a phone, began the 1/2 mile walk to the lodge. We were unsuccessful in reaching the motel for a ride and with our chins dragging the floor trying to decide what to do, a gentleman approached and asked if we were thru-hikers. We told him of our dilemma and he graciously offered us the use of a meeting room to sleep in for the night as well as a hot shower, then left for the evening turning the place over to us. Once again we were blessed with a trail angel when we needed it the most and spent a splendid evening in comfort as we watched a powerful thunderstorm pass by. Our boots and socks had been wet for quite a few days and Midnite had the brilliant idea of hanging our socks over the shower next to a heat lamp to dry them. Unfortunately, we inadvertently locked the bathroom door and were suddenly faced with a touchy situation - a small room with toxic socks 12 inches from a great source of heat and not being able to get in. We could smell our socks (mostly Midnite's socks) and were afraid the entire lodge would explode from the fumes. Luckily, we had Mr. Tuthill's business card and we sheepishly phoned him and told him of our predicament. He arrived shortly thereafter and was very good natured about being called away from home to rescue two smelly pair of socks from a locked shower room. We explained to him that not all thru-hikers were as hair-brained as we were and hoped that this episode would not keep him from sheltering another hiker.

We had our sights set on the hostel at Delaware Water Gap, Pennsylvania which was in the Presbyterian Church of the Mountain. The members of the church put on a potluck dinner for thru-hikers every Thursday night. "I've never been to a potluck," I said to Midnite, "We don't have them in South Africa." I was curious to experience one, and being a thru-hiker, food is always something to look forward to and anticipate. However, it turned out that we would get to Delaware Water Gap on Tuesday, and the potluck was on Thursday and we didn't really want to hang about all that time. I was disappointed, but was placated by a promise from Midnite that she, or her mom, would arrange a potluck for me when we returned to Ohio, so mollified by that, we left the next morning. But, the thought of all the food I was missing stayed with me for a few days, especially since I was eating pasta then!

The hostel was expected to be crowded as most everyone made it a point to be there on Thursday night and they would hang around for days to take part in this eating frenzy, so we decided to pitch our tents on the lawn behind the church. This too soon filled up so we escaped to a small gazebo in the front of the church for a peaceful night.

We were anxious to get back on the trail the next morning since we would be leaving Pennsylvania - seven states down, seven to go. The rocks, we heard, would soon diminish as we entered New Jersey and our feet were ready for a break.

CHAPTER 5

"YOU'RE GOING TO DO WHAT?"

Mel: *I had many reasons for wanting to attempt a thru-hike. The first time I stepped foot on the Appalachian Trail was in June 1993.   My brother Stephen, brother-in-law Terry and myself were out for a two day hike. This was my first backpacking trip and as I sat on the summit of the Priest Mountain and gazed into the valley below, the A.T. became a magical place to me. For the last year I had been rebuilding the life that had previously been taken from me by my eating disorder.   I was still not physically (my weight was at 100 pounds and I'm 5' 7") or mentally as strong as I would like to have been after a year in recovery, but I realized that I was beginning to feel freedom from its hold on me and up until that very moment I hadn't felt that. I also realized that with every pound that I gained I would become stronger and the stronger I became, the more I could hike, so in a way, the A.T. was therapy for me.   Over the next two years I would spend all of my vacation time backpacking different sections of the trail and with each trip I found it more and more difficult to return home and the nine to five world.*

My life was pretty stable and alot of people would say I had it all. A 36 year old, single homeowner, a wonderful family, a good job, nice car, friends, what else could I want? I often wondered that myself, but the sudden death of a very dear friend after a brief battle with cancer left me taking a very hard look at my life. Before her death, Joella and I would discuss my dream of "some day" thru-hiking the trail, something that seemed impossible to do at the time, but she would always encourage me to do it. She would always say, "Don't wait till tomorrow, tomorrow may never come." I remembered those words the more I thought of the trail, but how could I possibly quit my job and hike for six months, and what if I failed? When I admitted myself into the hospital for treatment I was told I was lucky to be alive. I had burned all the muscle in my body from constant

exercise including my heart. I was a time bomb waiting to
go off. I believe that God gave me a second chance on life for
a reason and as ridiculous as it may sound to some people, I
believe that reason was to hike the Appalachian Trail. I was
not going to blow my second chance on life. I was not going
to have anymore regrets in my life. My father told me when
I began my recovery that if I used the same determination
that I used to lose weight in regaining weight that I'd be just
fine. He was right and that same determination, I hoped,
would be with me on my hike.

I also looked forward to my hike to experience all the trail
had to offer. The natural beauty that would surround me
every day, the physical challenge having gone from not
being able to walk up a flight of stairs to carrying a 45
pound pack up a mountain, and all of the people I would
meet both on and off the trail. To live simply and
appreciate everything around me, the warmth of the sun
after a rain, the sounds of the birds at first light, and the
wonders that God had created.

Lindi: I don't know if my reasons for doing the trail are as
solid as Midnite's, but some of them are similar. Just
before I left South Africa, the sudden death of two
colleagues and the heartbreaking news of my 19 year old
nephew's death after a long illness, reinforced my decision
to go.

I have always been fascinated by American history,
particularly if it has anything to do with Native Americans,
and I have always wanted to live in America. Early America
must have been paradise, and I wanted to find a bit of that
paradise.

I was 46, I had a long standing relationship with my partner
Des, and a career as a graphic artist. We lived a simple,
almost idyllic life on the edge of the sea, in a small fishing
village almost on the tip of South Africa, but I have always
yearned for adventure and so I decided to follow my dream -
to seize the day. In the words of Henry David Thoreau: "I
went to the woods because I wanted to live deliberately, to

Appreciate the beauty of incompleteness - Zenwalker

want only the essential facts of life, and see if I could learn what it had to teach and not when I came to die, discover that I had not lived." Basically, I did it because I wanted to.

July 18th. Many things were changing the further north we headed and crossed into New Jersey. Unfortunately the food in our packs was the same. I carried three separate food bags - one held breakfast and dinners, one for lunch, and the third snacks. Everytime I opened one up I would say to Out of Africa, "Just once I wish something else would magically appear instead of what I KNOW is in here." We simply ate to live, we didn't live to eat and if hadn't been for the gnawing in our stomachs, we could have easily skipped meal time. The food was becoming very boring and basically all tasted the same, tasteless and bland and it only made matters worse knowing that we had three more months of the same. On this day we would encounter our first glacial pond, Sunfish Pond, that to us was as big as a lake and followed it for nearly an hour. The frogs put on quite a diving display as they jumped in front of us and into the water. We would continually ask each other, "What makes a pond a pond, and a lake a lake." We knew very little about the terrain in New Jersey but one thing was for sure, the ankle twisting rocks we had been hiking over the last few weeks were beginning to fade away much to our delight and it surprised us how wet and boggy New Jersey was.

One of the reasons we carried "Wingfoots" handbook was to help us in planning our re-supply stops and occasionally we would read that at a road crossing there would be a convenience store, etc., where we might have a break from the monotony of the contents of our food bags. This was the case at Culvers Gap and the 10.8 miles we hiked in a slight drizzle to the road did not phase us, as we were dreaming of Worthingtons Bakery and fresh, warm cinnamon rolls. The smell was incredible as we entered the store and we skipped all the packaged goodies, (sorry Little Debbie's) that we usually zeroed in on and made our way to the old wooden case filled with mouth watering pastries. Buying boring supplies was put on hold as we dashed outside to sit and enjoy our cinnamon rolls, smothered in icing. That evening at the Gren Anderson Shelter, our friends BoSox and

Snowman apparently didn't get their fill at Worthingtons as they packed in a whole apple pie for dessert.

We knew we were ready for a day off as we were both becoming edgy which always meant we were tired and hurting. Midnite's sister Lesa, was planning to meet us on the 22nd in Vernon, New Jersey at the Apple Valley Inn and we were looking forward to a day off and celebrating Lesa's birthday with her. We were given the royal treatment at the inn by Mitzi and John Durham in their three-story house and our tastebuds rejoiced as we were treated to some wonderful home cooking. It was obvious that thru-hikers had a smell all their own, but it was an odor that we never found particularly offensive and rarely did we notice it, but Lesa thought otherwise. We had been running errands in town and noticed four of our thru-hiker friends in front of (where else) a restaurant. They had hitched into town for supplies and were about to leave again for the trail and we offered them a ride. We would need to make two trips since they would not all fit in the van with their packs. As we dropped off the first two, Lesa immediately rolled down her window as we made our way back to town. We just assumed she was getting warm and thought nothing of it although it was a rather cool morning. After our second delivery to the trail, she commented that the odor was really overwhelming! We hadn't even noticed and wondered if WE smelled the same way when we climbed into someone's car when hitching into town, although we don't remember anyone ever rolling down their windows.

July 23rd we left Lesa behind and I left Vernon ready to hike. Once again, being with family made me terribly homesick and my attitude was that Out of Africa and I would start pulling big mile days and get home, unfortunately I didn't clue Out of Africa in on these feelings. We stepped foot out of the van and it began to rain. I was really fired up to hike and really didn't mind the rain as my focus was on getting to the New Jersey/New York line and entering another state. Out of Africa did not share in my enthusiasm and after hiking over 1,300 miles together, we had our first disagreement. She wanted to stop at the first shelter and call it a day after hiking less than six miles from Vernon. All I could think of was doing miles and she reluctantly agreed to go to the next shelter. Upon reaching the state line we had cleared the air and were glad to be in New York. Our exuberance was short lived as the rain continued and the rocks became larger and extremely slick. We encountered our first rock ladder that led us over huge boulders and was not anchored to the rock face and we could feel it sway as we climbed. I approached a vertical slab of rock about three feet in height and placed the toe of my left boot on the edge to step up. I knew when my right foot left the ground that I did not have a good foot hold and I was right. My foot slipped off and I slid head first down the face of the rock to the ground with all of my weight on my right hip and elbow. I was terrified that I had broken something and the position I was lying in would not allow me to unbuckle my hip belt so I could try and get up. Out of Africa raced to me and with trembling hands unbuckled my belt and helped me to my feet. Nothing felt broken except for my spirit and with some minor abrasions and shaky nerves, we moved on. The rest of the day would only get worse for me. I was terrified every time I placed my foot on a rock to step up and I began tripping and falling over the smallest root in the trail and each fall resulted in a bloody knee. With two miles left to the shelter I thought the day would never end and suddenly we were faced with a huge jumble of boulders. I promptly stopped and could not make my legs move to cross them. Out of Africa stepped into the lead and told me to follow her and I would be just fine. With tears streaming down my face I did as I was told. Finally after 19.7 miles, I limped into the shelter behind Out of Africa at 5:00 p.m. both of us cold, wet, and exhausted. My head was numb and I felt that the trials of the entire day were all my fault since it was I that wanted to push the miles. I kept thinking "if only" we had stopped earlier in the day none of this would have happened and felt I didn't deserve the kindness and support shown to me by Out of Africa. I would enter in my journal that night - "As I fell today I saw the last 3 1/2 months flash before me and figured it was all over for me." I believe that everything happens for a reason and this was a sign for me to slow down and enjoy the trail. Sleep did not come easily to me that night as every time I closed my eyes I saw myself falling from the rock ladder we had climbed earlier in the day. When sleep did overcome me, that same vision was in my dreams. In my next maildrop my mother, after hearing of my fall, sent a special inspirational saying to me. It read:

"For He orders His angels to protect you wherever you go. They will steady you with their hands to keep you from stumbling against the rocks on the trail." (Psalm 91: 11-12) She always seemed to find the right words to encourage me and give me strength. We had planned to do 14 miles the next day and felt none the worse the next morning as we crawled from our tents. We soon realized that the previous day had taken more out of us than we thought. I would approach each rock climb with fear rising up in my throat and as I had one foot firmly placed on a rock, it took all my strength and courage to lift the other from the security of the ground. It would have been so easy to turn around and walk the other way and say I can't do it, but instead I would cry and climb. After hiking 10 1/2 miles we decided that neither of us could go on and we spent the remainder of the day in our tents resting. As I lay in my tent, I prayed that this fear would leave me. Unfortunately it would remain with me the rest of our journey and only with God's help and Out of Africa's never ending support was I able to climb over rain slickened rocks.

We were finding New York difficult and were not alone in our thinking. Our fellow thru-hikers were also disgruntled with the terrain and the rocks, which made us feel somewhat better. I only had one lingering ache from my fall and that was in my hand which made it impossible to unbuckle my hipbelt and painful to use my hiking stick. We were beginning to realize that we would have to adjust our mileage as the terrain continued to be rocky and steep. Despite the small rocks in Pennsylvania we were mostly ridgerunning and were still able to put in 16 mile days, but now, for the first time in our hike, we would have to lower our daily mileage. I always felt as if we were regressing when we had to do that, but I had learned my lesson and was ready to adjust. Harriman State Park (despite the boulders) was beautiful with stands of hemlocks and open forest and for a change we were walking around the rocks, not over them. I was on a rollercoaster the next few days as my emotions ranged from fear to confidence. As I was approaching yet another rock climb, I could feel my throat tighten and my heart begin to race and suddenly the last words of a bible verse "Fear not for thou art with me" came to mind and brought me great comfort. From then on when anxiety would begin to take over, I would repeat those words over and over in mind and they would calm me.

On July 26th we trudged through a downpour to the Graymoor Friary in Peekskill, New York. The weather had turned hot and humid and the spring rains had brought the first onslaught of bugs, mostly in the form of mosquitoes. We were thrilled to be at the monastery which is run by Franciscan Friars and they have opened their doors to thru-hikers for 20 years. This was one of the places we both had looked forward to when we were planning and dreaming of our hike. Once again we were shown to a small, but comfortable room and greatly enjoyed a hot shower. Dinner was served promptly at 5:00 p.m. and we had a delightful conversation with Father Raymond. However, we were a bit disappointed that he wore ordinary clothes. We had this image in our minds (as most people do), of a silent monk, shuffling along in sandals, wearing a long, drab, robe. Out of Africa sat next to him, and said, "It's hard to know what to call you when you wear street clothes. I was expecting you to be wearing a monk robe." We felt rested the next morning and departed the Friary under sunny skies. We were beginning to think that things could not get any worse than they had been, but were mistaken as the mosquitoes made their appearance in swarms. It was futile to apply repellent as we would sweat it off in a matter of minutes. They were relentless flying in our eyes, nose, and ears. Anywhere that was exposed was fair game. We would try to hike as fast as we could in hopes of leaving them behind but it was impossible.

Out of Africa had been struggling the last few days as her paced slowed and her energy level plummeted. I was growing more concerned each day and by mid-morning I felt she needed to see a doctor. My biggest concern was lyme disease as ticks were plentiful and we had seen quite a few on us and our gear. Out of Africa is as head strong as I am and we would have a battle of wills in deciding whether to take a dirt road to the nearest town, or continue on the trail. I simply began hiking down the road and Out of Africa followed yelling her disapproval of the entire situation. I felt scared and frustrated when we finally stopped after a mile of road walking. We finally compromised with Out of

Africa agreeing that if she did not improve in the next few days, she would see a doctor.

I wasn't eating enough, although I didn't realize it at the time. I would be alright for a few hours and then I would get really tired and cranky. I often used to just stop and cry. I can't believe it now, its not like me at all, but I just felt that I couldn't go another step. Then I started to eat more. I would eat two or three granola bars before lunch, and even then by lunch I was a little testy. I remember catching up to Midnite one day and saying in a very frosty voice, "When do you intend stopping for lunch?" I don't think I ever really told Midnite, although I made a joke of it to others, but if I had reached the point of having to ask her that, then I was really on the edge and just had to stop! We often hiked 5-8 minutes apart, and although we couldn't see each other we knew we weren't far away. Sometimes, I would be thinking, "Why doesn't she stop? What's she doing?" So, by the time I caught her up, and she was sitting calmly on a log or rock, already with her bagel raised to her mouth, I was ready to do bodily harm! But, I was usually just happy to see my partner and I soon forgot I was cranky and lost no time in getting my pack off and lunch out. We were able to hitch a ride back to the trail by a kindly couple driving a Land Rover. Midnite told them of her concern for my health and before our departure they gave us their name and phone number instructing us to call them if we needed a ride or help finding medical help. Once again, a trail angel(s) was sent to us when we were in need.

The mosquitoes were descending on us in hordes and we were both beginning to feel tired and burned out. There was no escape from them. As quickly as we killed one, there would be ten more to come to the funeral. We would push ourselves as long and as hard as we could before giving in to take a quick break. When we dropped our packs they would swarm around them like bees to honey as they were drawn to the heat radiating from our packs and us. As we hiked we would wave our bandanas in front of our faces to give us some reprieve, but the rest of our body was left exposed and covered in bites. These blood suckers were relentless and would attack us as soon as we exited our tents in the morning and would stay with us until we crawled into them at night. We had picked up some mosquito coils that we would burn while cooking dinner which gave us some relief, but we could still hear them singing in our ears. Midnite said that being in a room full of hungry mosquitoes was worse than any Chinese water torture! It was becoming a mental struggle to put on our boots each morning and hike. It was impossible to enjoy the trail and we felt robbed of some beautiful country.

July 30th found us really jetsetting - breakfast in New York and lunch in Connecticut. This was our 10th state and we were welcomed to New England by a sign hanging on a huge birch tree. We were both happy to be in New England, despite the hordes of mosquitoes that still pestered us. We had hiked our first eight miles of the day along the beautiful Ten Mile River. We were headed into the lovely town of Kent to re-supply and it was typical New England. Full of people browsing in the quaint shops, and a couple stopped us and asked us where we had come from and where we were going, then wished us good luck. They didn't have a laundry in Kent so we had to do it by hand and try to dry it by hanging it on the railing outside our hotel room. Fortunately, the hikers room was at the back of the hotel. By evening, our clothes were still damp and we resorted to a new tactic - drying them with the aide of a hair dryer that we found in the bathroom. We also draped everything we could around the room utilizing the lamp shades, and the television set. After our errands were completed, we headed across the street for dinner. A car pulled up and two friends of Midnite's, Terry and Randy, poked their heads out of the window, waving madly. We were both really surprised. They were on their way to Maine for a vacation and had phoned Midnite's mother to find out where we were. They had been looking for us and it was a coincidence that as they were passing, we were walking down the street. We spent a pleasant evening in their company and Midnite was glad to see a familiar face from home.

We left Kent later than usual the next morning because of the rain, and because of that, another coincidence happened. As we were crossing the street, someone called "Hey Africa!" We looked up and saw Buzz walking down the street. We hadn't seen him for three weeks and we had a happy reunion. It was great to see him again, but hard to hug with our packs on. "I saw your messages to hurry up and catch you," he said. "I knew I would catch up with you guys either today or tomorrow." He had really caught us in Delaware Water Gap. He had hiked in at 10:30 p.m. the night we were there sleeping on the pavilion after he had hiked 28 miles! We said our "see you laters," and off we went. We would be descending St. Johns Ledges, a descent described in the handbook as "putting the hurt in your knees." "The area," according to the handbook, "is used by rock climbers to practice their art," which left us more than reluctant to tackle in the pouring rain. It held up to its reputation of leaving our knees screaming but was not nearly as bad as we expected. As often happened on our journey, we would dread a section of trail only to find it not nearly as difficult as we had heard or read about. "Expect the worse and be mentally prepared," was quickly becoming our credo.

We departed Silver Hill Campsite wet from rains the day before. My outlook on the day would be quite pessimistic each day that it would rain as my fear of wet rocks was not getting any better. My first clue that this would not be a good day was my emotions as we approached Hatch Brook. It wasn't a wide stream, but was running moderately fast and the trail crossed it via a wide and very slippery log. "I can't do this," I told Out of Africa, "I just can't cross that log." I felt the panic heighten as I looked for a safer way to cross, but to no avail. I paced back and forth along the bank feeling like a caged animal. Out of Africa calmly suggested that we take off our boots and socks and wade across as it was a sandy bottom with good footing. I felt as if someone had hit me in the head with a brick. Lately, when confronted with a difficult situation, my logical thought process would become confused, and obvious solutions to a problem would vanish as fear took over. Luckily for me, Out of Africa had all her faculties. I was finding it increasingly difficult to think rationally. My mental state of mind was on the fragile edge of disaster and I would spend a large part of the day in tears, or on the verge of tears. My body was tired and my energy level low.

I felt quite proud of myself for fording our first stream (crossing water without the aid of rocks or footbridge) and my optimism for a good day returned, but it was short lived. We continued for another couple of miles and I suddenly slipped and twisted my ankle. "Out of Africa," I cried out, "Help me!" I had felt it lock and could not put any weight on it to help myself up from the ground. I was totally frustrated. "I bet you're getting tired of helping me off the ground" I commented to Out of Africa. I was certainly getting tired of being there. I was able to hike the mile to the nearest road and waited as Out of Africa went for help. As much as I hated to go to the hospital, there was also a part of my exhausted mind that said, "If it's broken, you'll have to go home." My tears, while waiting along side the road, were from pain and those thoughts. I wasn't ready to quit, but I was too tired to realize it. Upon locating a phone, Out of Africa dialed 911 and within minutes an emergency squad arrived to transport me to the hospital in Salisbury, Connecticut. The x-rays revealed that it was a severe sprain and I was told that I could continue to hike, but it would take longer to heal. I also found out that I had a stress fracture in the ball of my foot, that I assumed, was left over from the rocks in Pennsylvania, but there was nothing they could do for it. This bit of information I did not reveal to Out of Africa until a few days later. I figured since I was already there I would have my hand and wrist x-rayed as it continued to hurt from my fall in New York. Again, it was a bad sprain and I was taped up and sent on my way.

Sitting on the curb outside the emergency room door, Out of Africa and I discussed what we should do. My heart was not ready to go back on the trail, but the lodging in Salisbury was not within a thru-hikers budget. We felt we had no other recourse but to return to the trail. The door to the hospital opened and one of the nurses exited carrying Out of Africa's bandana that she had left in the emergency room. We asked if she knew of an inexpensive place we might stay for the night and she shook her head negatively but said she would check with the other nurses as she did not live in the immediate area. She soon returned with an angel in a nurse's uniform by the name of Madaline. "I get off work at 3:30 and you can come home with me, take showers, do your laundry, and stay the night." she said. Once again, a miracle had happened. After a stop at the grocery store we were told to make ourselves at home as Madaline left us, saying she was going to pick blueberries and would be back in a couple of hours, two total strangers in her home. Madaline told us we could stay as long as we wanted to. She was very concerned about Midnite, and told us before we left that if we thought we needed to stay longer, we would be very welcome to do so.

I knew deep down inside that I needed to take some time off and rest, but did not want to admit that I was exhausted to myself or Out of Africa.   Pride is a terrible thing sometimes.   I guess I figured that if I pushed myself hard enough we would finish sooner and THEN I could rest.   I wrote in my journal that night - "I'm ready to quit, I can't take the fear anymore.   Everytime it rains and I see wet rocks my chest gets tight and the fear is unbelievable.   My head isn't in it anymore, but my heart still is.   I feel so tired, physically and mentally and I know I need to rest but I also feel pressure of doing miles." After a long discussion on the phone with my mother about my mental state of mind, Out of Africa and I decided that we would go back to the trail the next morning. We planned to do a really short day, just a mile or two and rest the remainder of the day.   I promised myself and my mother that we would take it easy. As my head rested on a real pillow that night, I knew that it would be difficult to live up to that promise, for once I was back on the trail, I wanted to hike.   Madaline graciously drove us back to the trail, and we couldn't thank her enough for all her kindness and generosity.   The first shelter was 1.3 miles from the road and upon arrival we decided that it wasn't all that nice a place to spend the day.   After a brief rest, we struggled another 2.6 miles to Sharon Mountain Campsite, which was equally as depressing and meant we would have to spend the day in our tents because the mosquitoes were horrible.   Once again, the packs went on our backs and we hiked another 2.9 miles to Belter Campsite, all the while the guilt of breaking my promise to myself was overwhelming - a real battle of the mind.   I knew I should be resting, but was pushing myself over the edge and could feel it coming.   My ankle was not giving me too much trouble so I figured, keep hiking.   Belter Campsite was as bad as the first campsite and the next shelter was 6.2 miles away.   At this point it wouldn't have made any difference if it was 20 miles away, my brain seemed to quit functioning altogether. It was as if my body was on

*Fear knocked on the door, Faith answered and
there was no one there*

automatic pilot and despite the hordes of mosquitoes, I just swatted, cried and hiked my way to Limestone Springs Lean-To. The 1.3 mile day I had hoped for quickly turned into 13.2 miles of hell. Upon reaching the side trail to the shelter we discovered a note from Elf that said the half mile trail to the shelter was ridiculous and that the shelter area was plagued with mosquitoes. We were both so tired we figured it couldn't be that bad, but soon found it to be as bad or worse than Elf had reported. We turned around, found a level spot, and pitched our tents. I was at my lowest point since beginning the trail and found it difficult to discuss it with Out of Africa. My journal for August 2nd read - "New England is probably the toughest part of the A.T. and maybe I don't feel I can do it despite what I've already done. Where has my courage gone? Did I leave it on that rock in New York? And where has my determination and drive gone?" All I could think of as I drifted off to sleep was quitting and going home.

August 3rd dawned as it had the last few mornings, with the sound of mosquitoes zipping in our ears the minute we stepped outside our tents. I think I knew as soon as I picked up my pack that I would go no further than Salisbury, our re-supply stop 4.2 miles away. Out of Africa was ready to go before I was and I sent her on saying I would catch up. Every step was painful, not physically, but mentally as I knew that I had to break the news to Out of Africa that I was leaving the trail. How could I let her down by quitting? How would I feel if she decided not to go on because I wasn't? What about all the people at home supporting and cheering for me to succeed, how will I look in their eyes - a failure? I suddenly realized all these questions I was asking myself concerned everyone else, not me. I had told myself before I left home that if I weren't enjoying the hike and my heart wasn't in it that it was time to go home. It wasn't worth pushing myself physically or mentally to complete the trail, just to say I had finished it. The big question was, how to break it to Out of Africa, my friend, my partner, my lifeline. We stopped at the edge of town for a break and I began crying before I could drop my pack. I think Out of Africa knew what I was going to say before I opened my mouth. "The fire has gone out," I told her, "I can't go on like this any longer." "We only have 600 more miles to go to Katahdin" she said fighting back the tears. "That would be like telling someone who hated to hike that they had to backpack 600 miles when they knew it would be miserable, I just can't do it," I replied, tears streaming down my face. For the first time, I realized that Out of Africa would not be able to help me when I said "I Can't." We went miserably into town, discussing her options of going on. I was relieved that she was going to continue, but also knew that saying goodbye would be heartbreaking. We knew that our friend Buzz was ahead of us by a day, two days at the most, and upon reaching Salisbury, decided the best thing for her to do would be to jump ahead a few miles and catch up to him. After a phone call home, I made arrangements to go by bus to Pennsylvania and meet my mom and sister, and they would drive me home. We were lucky to run in to Attitude and his wife who was helping him slackpack a few days. She offered to drive Out of Africa back to the trail in hopes of catching up with Buzz today or tomorrow. Goodbyes are never easy and this one was the hardest I ever had to say. We had been together night and day for four months and suddenly Out of Africa would turn her back and walk up the trail without me. "I'll see you in Maine," she whispered as we hugged goodbye, "I want you to meet me and climb Katahdin with me." "There is no way I can do that," I told her, "I won't have earned that right." I had already convinced myself that I was a failure, despite the fact that I had hiked nearly 1,500 miles. My heart broke in two as she shouldered her pack, turned, and walked away, never looking back.

Mel: *My only option for lodging in Salisbury was at an expensive inn, but I needed somewhere to stay and promptly checked in. I spent most of the afternoon lying on the bed trying to convince myself that I had made the right decision. Despite the support I was receiving from my family that it was ok to come home, it still did not feel right. My journal entry partially read - "The fire has gone out and I will be taking a bus to Pennsylvania tomorrow to meet mom and Lesa, then home. I woke up this morning and the feelings of dread returned that have been there since New York. I can't explain it, but it boils down to everything being gone, the zest, the excitement of what is ahead, and the anticipation. The last few weeks I have been fighting for Lindi's sake. 600 miles left to go. Why couldn't I just keep pushing on."*

Midnite

Out of Africa

April 5 - Weighing Packs - Amicalola Falls State Park, GA

May 4 - Bald Mountain, Tennessee

May 19 - Troutdale, Virginia

June 19 - Out of Africa & Buzz, Pass Mountain Shelter, VA

June 25 - The Disciples, Rat, Buzz-David Lesser Shelter, VA

June 26 - A. T. Conference H.Q.- Harpers Ferry, W. Virginia

June 29 - Out of Africa - Weverton Cliffs, Maryland

July 2 - Midnite - Quarry Gap Shelter, Pennsylvania

July 23 - Out Of Africa - Rocks in New York

August 15 - Baker Peak, Vermont

August 25 - Out of Africa, Mr. Bean, Hiking Vikings,
Midnite, Cruiser Canuk - Mt. Moosilauke, NH

August 31 - Midnite-Mt. Washington (White Mountains), NH

September 7 - Welcome to Maine

September 18 - Kennebec River, Maine

October 1 - Midnite, Out of Africa, Bandana Light, McCoy,
Casper, Mountain Lion, Dead Man Walking, Gypsy
Mt. Katahdin, Maine

Early evening found me still stretched across the bed and suddenly a vision of Upper Goose Pond Cabin entered my mind. This cabin was a place that Out of Africa and I had been looking forward to once we entered Massachusetts. I tried to push it out of my mind. I know how my mind operates, and once it starts on something its like a runaway freight train. The harder I tried to dismiss it, the stronger it kept coming back and the next thing I knew I was on my feet and standing in front of the hotel desk. I asked the clerk how I could make arrangements to get to the nearest road to Upper Goose Pond Cabin. I had given Out of Africa the trail maps and data book that I carried, but felt sure that the cabin wasn't more than two or three miles from Goose Pond Road. The plan I was formulating in my mind was to hike to the cabin, rest, and wait for Out of Africa to arrive the next day or at the most two days. Up until this point we had been purists, which meant that we made it a point to hike past every blaze of the white-blazed trail. This would mean I would have to skip a section of the trail. Weighing the difference of quitting, or missing a few miles that I could make up later, the purist option went out the window. For the first time in weeks I felt positive and motivated and when I called my mother (for the 20th time that day) she was supportive and glad for my decision to try it again. Before I hung up from talking with her there was a knock at my door and to my surprise it was my friends Terry and Randy (whom we had seen in Kent). Once again they had called my mother inquiring to my whereabouts. They were within an hour's drive of Salisbury and came to my rescue on hearing the news I was leaving the trail. Terry and I had a long discussion about my state of mind and she encouraged me (as she had before I started the trail) to continue. The last piece of my plan was in place as they offered to drive me to Goose Pond Road the next morning. I knew in my heart that it was meant for me to continue and anxiously awaited morning.

The next morning I was up early as I still needed to re-supply and get my gear together before Terry and Randy arrived. It was a beautiful sunny day, and after I said farewell to my friends, I eagerly began my 2.7 mile hike to the cabin. For the first time in weeks there were no mosquitoes and everything seemed right with the world except for the fact that Out of Africa had no idea I was back on the trail and I was in hopes that her spirits had lifted somewhat so that she too could enjoy this gorgeous day. I wished I could yell at the top of my lungs "Out of Africa, I'm back."

Upper Goose Pond Cabin was everything I had pictured it to be. A beautiful cabin situated on the banks of a crystal clear pond. I was greeted at the cabin by Octavia, the caretaker, and I told her that I might be there for two nights as I needed to rest and wait for my partner. "You've come to the right place" she said, and I soon found that she was right. I spent the remainder of the day sleeping and sitting on the deck next to the pond. Although it was (and always has been) difficult for me to sit still, I knew my body needed the rest. It was like old home week at the cabin as friends I had not seen in a long time made there way to the cabin, some to stay the night, others to take a break and move on.   McGyver, whom I hadn't seen since North Carolina, was hiking with June Bug and her brother Tree; Odysseus, Wayah and Bannor.   The first words out of everyone's mouth was "Where's Out of Africa," and word was quickly travelling of my return to the trail.   I didn't expect Out of Africa to make it to the cabin this day, but still watched the trail intently as hikers approached. Tomorrow, for sure, I hoped.

Octavia and I were up early the next morning to prepare pancakes for the thru-hikers, something that is routinely done by the caretaker. I have never mixed and cooked so many pancakes in my entire life. Everytime we turned around there was another empty plate waiting to be filled as thru-hikers stomachs are bottomless pits. How enjoyable it was to feed an appetite that was sick and tired of oatmeal. The remainder of the day was spent helping Octavia retrieve spring water via a canoe from across the lake, and sleeping. I don't believe I have ever slept as much as I did those two days. The more rest I got, the clearer my head became and my thought process quickly returned to normal. The day seemed to last forever and as evening approached I feared that Out of Africa would not arrive before dark. I didn't know if I could wait one more day to see her. I had resolved myself to the fact that she had stopped short of the cabin and I walked to the pond.   Upon my return I saw Buzz approaching the cabin and though I was thrilled (as always) to see him, my first words were "Where's Out of Africa?" We hugged and he told me he knew I couldn't go home and then said the words I had been waiting to here, "She's right behind me." My eyes did not move from the trail until I finally saw her red pack and I bolted towards her. In my excitement all I could think to say was "Where have you been?" She was exhausted as she and Buzz had hiked 21 miles over some difficult terrain to reach the cabin once they had heard through the trail grapevine that I had returned to the trail. "I couldn't quit" I told her as we embraced. The void I had been feeling over the last two days was suddenly gone as my partner and I were reunited. We both knew the toughest part of the trail was yet to come in the form of the White Mountains in New Hampshire, but I felt positive again and was ready to tackle the next 600 miles.

Lindi: I was totally unprepared for Mel's bombshell that she was leaving the trail. It stopped me in my tracks when she told me she would be staying in Salisbury. I think my first thoughts were for myself. What would I do without her? I knew she hadn't been happy for awhile, but I didn't know to what extent her spirits had sunk. I really misread the whole thing and if I had been more interested in my partner than in myself, perhaps it may not have happened. Though in retrospect, things did work out well and perhaps we needed the break from each other. It showed us how much we relied on one another.

I thought at first that Midnite just meant that she needed time to rest. When she said, as we were walking into Salisbury, "that she couldn't go any further," I couldn't believe it and I just started to cry. I wasn't ready to give up yet, and I knew Midnite wouldn't want me to stop, yet, the thought of going on without her made me sad. Many people do the trail alone and I'm sure I could have done it solo as well, but we had started the trail together long before we actually set foot on it, and I wanted us to finish together as well. I had always seen us standing together on Katahdin, and I was sure that somehow we would be up there together.

Attitude, Grey Wolf, Casper, and their wives were also in Salisbury and Vicki, Attitude's wife, offered to take me to the trail after dropping off Attitude and company who were slackpacking for a few days. Salisbury was also where I started smoking. I hadn't smoked for five years and although I was a social smoker and found it easy to stop, I couldn't believe it when I took it up again. For the rest of our journey I looked forward to it everytime we stopped. The day after we arrived in Millinocket, (after we had climbed Katahdin,) I stopped again and I have not had one since. Many hikers either started smoking or started smoking again while on the trail.

Vicki dropped me off at the trailhead, we hugged and I thanked her, then I turned to my partner. What was there to say? She walked a little way with me. It seemed unreal, like a dream. In a moment I would walk away on my own. After spending every day of four months in her company and walking 1,474 miles with her, she wasn't coming with me. I could hardly see the trail for tears.

I was on my way to Glen Brook Shelter where I hoped to catch Buzz, but to be honest, at that moment I didn't really care. I left a note in the trail which told him I was at the shelter and needed to talk to him. I was glad to see him. He dropped his pack and said "What's up Africa?" I told him, with a catch in my voice, that Midnite was off the trail. He and Wharf Rat, who was also there, looked at me incredulously. "I can't believe it," they both kept saying. Buzz came to sit beside me in the shelter and placed an arm around my shoulder. "Don't worry Africa, if you need a partner we can hike together for awhile." Buzz, as usual, came through. He had not planned to stop at the shelter, until I, by leaving my note, asked him to stop. I hiked with him for the next two days and although I missed Midnite, I did have an adventure!

I spent the evening in the company of Buzz, Jeff, and Greg of the Disciples, Lazy, Wharf Rat and of course, the mosquitoes. We built a fire and sat around talking and laughing at Jeff's stories. Midnite wasn't far from my thoughts and I missed seeing her sitting there with us. Someone had suggested going to Shea's Irish Pub for lunch the next day. It was four-tenths of a mile from where the trail crossed the road. Midnite and I probably wouldn't have stopped there, we would have made it to the road crossing much earlier. Before we went to our tents for the night, Buzz asked, "You want to go to Shea's tomorrow Africa?" "Sure" I said, "it will be a change."

Midnite and I were always on the trail by 6:00 or 6:30 in the morning and it didn't always make us popular in the shelters. Somehow our reputation for early rising preceded us and we were often greeted with, "Oh, so you're Midnite and Out of Africa, you like to get up early!" At 6:00 a.m. most of the guys I was with now were still asleep, but the camp was beginning to stir, scratching and yawning by 6:30, and by 8:00, Buzz and I were on the trail. We started off at an easy pace, but as it became hotter, the mosquitoes were out in force, and we all made it in record time through a large boggy area, and one by one met at the road. The others said they were going to take a short cut and follow the road. Buzz and I were purists and we said we would follow the white blazes and set out. We followed a dirt road for a while before coming to a relocation and a map pinned to a tree by the local maintaining club. The area was flooded and the map showed a relocation following the road that hikers should follow. That is, everyone but Buzz. "Can't be that bad," he said, leaving the road and following the trail into the woods. "Comin?" he called back. I shrugged, what the heck, I thought. It was a pleasant walk through the woods for about 45 minutes, and then Buzz stopped in his tracks. "Oh," I heard him say, and laugh a little. "It is flooded isn't it," he said. "Shall we take out boots off?" I asked. "You must be joking," he said, "I'm not walking through that in bare feet." He was already standing up to his ankles in water on the first plank. The trail crews put bridges across bogs for hikers to walk on made of thick wood. "Walk where I walk Africa," he called. Every time he stepped on a plank I had to wait for it to come to the surface again so I could see it. "Come on" he was laughing. "All right for you," I called, "You're 6 feet 4, I'm only 5 foot 2." I nearly lost my boots twice, slipping off the plank, or I thought, looking into the mucky water, pulled by some bog creature. It took ten minutes to get across. Wet and muddy we made it to the other side and finally to the road. We squished our way up to the pub, laughing about the bog, and the water, which at times had been up to my knees. The others were already there. We took our wet boots, socks and gaiters off and left them in the sun to dry.

We were still sitting around the table at 1:30 p.m., but by 2:00 we reckoned it was time to make a move. We still had five miles to hike to Tom Leonard Shelter. Hiking after a heavy lunch is not my favorite thing to do and Midnite and I never did it. Plagued once again by mosquitoes, Buzz surged ahead, and I found myself hiking alone, well, me and the mosquitoes! I caught up with Buzz and the others just before the shelter and we finally arrived at 6:00 p.m. that evening. Kevin and Stephen, the other half of the Disciples, staggered in just before full dark. They had also been to the pub and had spent a lazy few hours there.

The next morning, I woke at the usual time and got out the books to see where we would end up that night. Upper Goose Pond was 21 miles away. It was a place that both Midnite and I wanted to visit. Buzz joined me later to ask what I wanted to do. We decided that we would "shoot" for Upper Goose Pond and if it proved too much, we would camp on the way. The mosquitoes were out again, and by now my arms and back were covered in bites. I was also prone to getting scratched by briars. Sometimes I would have two or three deep scratches that flowed with blood. I looked like I had been in a cat fight. We stopped for an early lunch at 11:30 at Mt. Wilcox South Shelter. Since Buzz cooked his lunch, I was ready to go before him and told him I would see him along the trail, knowing he would probably catch me up. I came upon Jeff and Lazy sitting in the trail, almost dozing in the sun. Jeff should have been with Greg in Tyringham meeting Greg's brother. "Did you see Midnite?" Jeff asked me. I was confused. "Midnite?" I asked, "No, why, should I?" But something fluttered inside me. I refused to be hopeful. "I'm not messing with you," Jeff said. "We saw Attitude, and he said Midnite was at Wilcox Shelter." "Well, we were just there and she wasn't there" I said, keeping my voice and face unemotional. It's easy, being British! "I went down to Wilcox North Shelter" Jeff said, "She wasn't there either, and no message." Buzz walked up and we told him, his eyebrow went up. I knew if she was anywhere, she would be at Upper Goose Pond. Buzz and I set off again, leaving Jeff and Lazy sitting in the shade.

Sometime during the afternoon, it had been agreed that we would try for Upper Goose Pond. We still had ten miles to hike. "At a leisurely two miles an hour," Buzz said, "We'll *be there by 7:00 p.m." He forgot to add that he was 27, and as I've said, 6' 4". I was a few years older, and with much shorter legs! Buzz once again put on his mosquito pace and I was left behind. I hardly ate and I was hungry and thirsty. I didn't want to stop and be swarmed by the mosquitoes. It was really miserable. Eventually, at 7:35 p.m., nearly dark, I saw the sign for Upper Goose Pond, and with a sigh, turned up the side trail. I completely missed a note that Midnite had left for me on the trail. I soon saw lights and heard voices, then a figure came hurdling towards me, and I dropped my pack just before Midnite threw her arms around me. (I've read her version, but what she actually said was), "You little shit, you pulled a 21 mile day." It was 7:45 p.m., and Buzz had been there for 45 minutes. I was exhausted and flopped down beside him on the porch. The evening was velvet soft. People waved and said Hi. Buzz smiled, "She kissed my hair," he told me. He hadn't washed it for some time. "She's brave," I said. He was sitting crossed legs, cooking his supper. I put my arms around him and kissed his cheek, "Thanks for being with me," I whispered in his ear. "Oh," he said, "you're welcome."*

I had left it up to Out of Africa whether she wanted to hike the next day or stay at the cabin and rest, but she suggested we just do a short day after a leisurely morning. I was more than happy to jump back into the kitchen and fix pancakes for my partner and Buzz, who helped her make it back to me. They were equally as delighted to eat them. Out of Africa took a brief swim in the pond and we were ready to hit the trail again. It was such a wonderful feeling to know she was walking behind me again and I felt our friendship would take a new direction after all the stress it had been under over the last few weeks. I believe everything happens for a reason and my indecision as to whether to continue on the trail forced us to realize how much we needed each other and made us appreciate each other again. It is a bit ironic that today was the day we decided to try and write a book about our journey when we completed the trail. I had thought before our journey began that I would like to attempt a story about my eating disorder and coming full circle in my life to do the trail. We figured, since we hiked together, we should write a book together. The title was obvious to us as we were continuing our journey of friendship. We were enjoying our hike and were within a mile or so of October Mountain Lean-To when I caught the toe of my boot on a root and suddenly found myself on my knees. As I fell, I twisted my knee and felt it lock on me and I fought back the tears as the previous weeks came flooding back to me. Out of Africa was by my side in an instant and said, "Why can't these things happen to me." I guess she figured I would go off the deep end again. I was able to stand and it felt fine once I was on my feet, so, I dusted myself off, gathered my pride, and we hiked on to the shelter, together, as it should be, side by side.

We were scheduled for another maildrop in Dalton, Massachusetts, and Out of Africa was looking forward to stretching out on the bed of our motel and channel surfing the television, her favorite pastime when we were in town. We were surprised to have a visit from the Disciples and Buzz. They wanted to stop and tell Midnite how happy they were she was back on the trail and offer some encouragement to her. Buzz told of us how frustrating it was becoming to him to never have his appetite satisfied and added another "Buzz story" to his repertoire. It seems after we left him at Upper Goose Pond Cabin, he decided to ride into town with Octavia, the caretaker, who was going for supplies. He had been craving pizza in the worst way and decided to try and fill his hollow leg. He promptly located a Pizza Hut and set about consuming 17 slices! He told us that he felt so ill after finishing his feast that he had to lie down on the floor in the middle of the restaurant. At least he couldn't say he was still hungry.

We had been hiking in glorious sunshine for a few days and much to our dismay we watched the dark clouds roll in as we ascended Mt. Greylock, the highest point in Massachusetts. We briefly stopped at Bascom Lodge for Out of Africa to buy postcards (another of her favorite things to do), then began the steep descent. We were about a mile from the small town of North Adams when the rain began, so we put our heads down and assumed our rain pace. As usual, the harder we hiked, the harder it rained and when we reached the road, our boots were overflowing with water. We spotted an elementary school with a large porch and dashed under it

It is only in stretching beyond what you ever dreamed you could do that you discover how high you can soar

until the rain subsided. Buck-Buck soon joined us and we decided to head to the Pizza Hut in town until things dried off a bit. We all had had our fill of hiking in the rain. We entered the front door, and was greeted by McGyver, a napkin draped over his arm, and he announced, "Good afternoon, my name is Donnie and I will be your waiter today." That alone would have been humorous enough, but he was dressed a little unusual, even for a thru-hiker. He and his companions, June Bug and Tree, had gone to the laundromat prior to the Pizza Hut. The only clothes McGyver could find to borrow while his trail clothes were washing, was a pair of mens pajamas that buttoned down the front. He was perfectly comfortable parading around in them while visiting the all-you-can-eat pizza bar.

CHAPTER 6

VERMONT, AUGUST 10, 1996

We crossed into our 13th state and joined the Long Trail, another long distance trail that extends north to the Canadian border. For the next 103 miles we would be hiking two trails simultaneously. We were beginning to climb up some pretty steep terrain, something we hadn't done for quite some time. It was amazing how quickly we got used to the rolling terrain in Pennsylvania, New Jersey, and New York, but now we would begin conditioning for the mountains that would lie between here and Katahdin. The days and nights were beginning to cool off which was a blessing, as far as the mosquitoes were concerned, but I wasn't quite ready for cold weather yet. I wouldn't be getting my cold weather gear until we reached the White Mountains. Out of Africa carried her down filled winter sleeping bag the entire trip so she was prepared for this early cold snap. One of the finest views afforded us from a shelter was at Goddard Shelter which sits almost at the summit of Glastenbury Mountain. From the covered veranda, the views south towards Mt. Greylock are some of the most spectacular on the trail. We arrived about 1:30 p.m. on a warm, sunny day, with scattered white clouds in a bright blue sky. Pines framed the mountains, blue with distance. We sat looking until it was too dark to see. This is what we had walked 1,600 miles to see. It was worth every step.

We had promised each other when we left Upper Goose Pond Cabin that we would try and keep our mileage low through the difficult sections and relax and enjoy these last few hundred miles. We left Goddard Shelter with the intention of staying at a ski patrol hut atop Stratton Mountain which was 16.3 miles away. The climb up Stratton Mountain looked to be steep according to the profile map, but we resolved that we would take our time and not push ourselves. We had heard that the hut was fully enclosed and had hot and cold running water. We did as we said we would and took it slow and easy as we made our way to the top and enjoyed some spectacular views on the way up. The ski patrol hut is (for obvious reasons) not used during the summer months, but is kept open for thru-hikers to use. We didn't mind doing a few extra miles when we knew what amenities awaited us at the end of the day. We were joined that night by some of our buddies, including Buck-Buck, whom we had first met in the bar at the Back Track Inn in Unionville, New York. We had hiked 20 miles when we arrived at the Inn at 1:30 p.m., and thereafter, Buck-Buck would always refer to it. He thought it was a fantastic feat. He also said, "that Midnite and I should carry lunch boxes and wear hard hats because we hardly had any time off, and he laughed that we were always up at the crack of dawn and off to work." Buck-Buck always wore an old hat and dark glasses, and because of his knee gaiters, had a very distinctive, cowboy-like gait. We had met Odysseus way back in Georgia, and every so often he would pop up again. Stretch and Bannor were fairly new to us but were fast becoming good trail buddies. It was quite windy and cold on top of Stratton Mountain and we were glad to have four walls surrounding us.

We were looking forward to a day off at Manchester Center, Vermont. It had been quite awhile since Out of Africa had taken a full non-hiking day and her knees were in constant pain. We had stretched our food bags the last few days to avoid an extra town visit before reaching Manchester Center and couldn't wait to get to town and eat. We constantly craved fresh fruit, vegetables and salads. We had heard a great deal about the hostel run by the Zion Episcopal Church and it certainly lived up to its rave reviews. Hikers were permitted to sleep on the floor of a large meeting room and we also had use of a well equipped kitchen as well as a sitting room complete with books, magazines, and VCR. We were like one big happy family and we met several hikers that we had been following for months in the trail registers: The Hiking Vikings, a couple from Minnesota; Lemstar, Gearmaster and Merlin. We were also reunited with Rat who by this time had changed his trail name to Peter Pan, but once a Rat always a Rat to us. We hadn't seen him since Harpers Ferry, WV, and he was finishing the trail without his dog Tyco as he had developed problems with his paws. The Disciples, minus David who left the trail at Harpers

Ferry, Buzz, McGyver, June Bug, Tree, and Sissyphus rounded out the familiar faces we hadn't seen for a while.

After hiking 500 miles to Damascus, Virginia, in the Hi-Tech boots Out of Africa brought from South Africa, she decided that she'd had enough of slipping and sliding in the mud and stones, and it was time to buy a new pair. There wasn't much of a choice in her size at the outfitter in Damascus, but she decided on a pair of leather Asolo. She carried her old Hi-Tech boots with her until we met our support team - Midnite's parents - at Troutdale, Virginia. She walked 15 miles in them the first day with only slight discomfort. They lasted almost another 1,175 miles. Two days before we got to Manchester Center, the sole on the right boot parted company from the upper, and not even duct tape would work to keep them together. It made walking very difficult. At Manchester Center she rang Asolo customer service and they told her she could go along to the outfitter and if they thought the sole should have lasted longer, she could have a new pair of boots. After the staff at the outfitter rang Asolo, she was given another pair of boots for a cost of $3.00, the difference between the styles. This time she took a bigger size, and although they looked big, there was plenty of room for her toes. They were much more comfortable. Out of Africa also met a Native American, a Cherokee, in Manchester Center. He asked her what trail we were hiking and they chatted for a while. She was really pleased to meet a Native American and after a while, he brought over a Walkman cassette player for her. He handed it to her with a smile, and said, "To keep you company on the trail." What a wonderful act of kindness from a stranger.

August 16th blessed us with some of the prettiest trail in Vermont. The terrain was relatively flat with gradual ascents, surrounded by beautiful tall pines and no undergrowth. Smaller pines hugged the trail which was covered by a thick bed of pine needles. It was like walking on carpet and we cruised along letting the warm breeze blow all our cares away. We decided to push a few more miles than we had planned and stay at Clarendon Shelter which would give us an 18.6 mile day - more than we wanted to do as we were still trying to keep mileage low, but the day was young and we were feeling good. We passed Clarendon Gorge and stood on the suspension bridge and watched some of the area residents swimming in the sparkling clear water. We were beginning to tire a little, but felt we had enough kick left to cover the 1.3 miles to the shelter. As we were quickly becoming aware, the terrain could change at the drop of a hat, and the last mile was a climb straight up. We were nearly out of water and it was the hottest part of the day which made it even tougher. All our feet wanted was to be released from their prison in the form of our boots and be free. The shelter was empty when we arrived but we were soon joined by Shaka, and Cruiser Canuk. Shaka was by far one of the most interesting thru-hikers we had met in a long time. He walked into the shelter carrying a paper bag containing a six pack of beer (which he gladly shared), and a box of doughnuts that he had purchased at the last road crossing. Shaka was truly one of a kind. He wore a kilt, which was nothing more than a piece of tartan material wrapped around his waist and secured with a pin. He claimed he enjoyed the freedom it gave him and swore it made hiking easier. Whatever the reason, he was certainly brave. He almost lost the whole thing on top of Mt. Washington as it was really blowing a gale and Shaka was trying to readjust his kilt for modesty. We found the whole thing very amusing. Cruiser Canuk was a strong, French Canadian hiker from Quebec. He had long, dark hair and a well toned body. It was a delight to listen to him speak in his beautiful French accent. We were treated that evening to a downpour of rain and the next morning doughnuts compliments of Shaka.

Our intentions were to go to The Inn at Long Trail as most everyone was headed there, but first we had to get up and over Killington Peak. The rain the night before had left the trail extremely muddy and we were feeling a little tired from our big miles the day before. We left the shelter faced with a moderate climb and then began the climb up Killington. For the next 4.1 miles we climbed up and over rocks (wet of course), with tree roots jutting out everywhere and mud up to our ankles. The trail was quite narrow and followed the edge of a ridge, so there was no room to maneuver and we had no choice but to stumble over all that was put in our path. It seemed to go on forever and we were pretty well wiped out when we stopped for lunch but still had not reached the summit. We decided rather than push on to the Inn that we would instead stop at Pico Camp for the night, an enclosed cabin that reportedly had excellent views. We reached the summit soon after lunch and stopped for a quick break next to Cooper Lodge, an old stone building that was used as a shelter. Lemstar, Cruiser Canuk and Shaka were already there taking a break and when we approached them Lemstar commented "Not too bad of a climb." I glanced at Out of Africa and in my leg weary state replied, "Compared to What!" It was difficult to stay at Pico Camp despite the breathtaking views of birch trees, pines and the early colors of the changing leaves in the valley below, as everyone who passed by headed on to the Inn. After a break we discussed pushing on. I was afraid of falling into the same routine that had exhausted Out of Africa and me a few short weeks ago and strongly suggested we stay put. It was always easy to say to ourselves "just another mile or so, it won't be too bad," but the "just another miles" would catch up with us sooner or later. We decided to kick back and enjoy having the shelter all to ourselves.

We were constantly on the lookout for moose as we had been hearing reports from other hikers of frequent sightings. We figured that it wouldn't be too difficult to see them since they were such large animals. As we climbed a gradual hill one afternoon, I noticed a movement in the woods to my left and assumed it was a deer. I stopped and looked behind me to see where Out of Africa was and as I turned back around I was surprised to find that it wasn't a deer, but in fact a young moose. I knew Out of Africa would be disappointed to miss seeing it but I also knew that if I yelled at her to hurry it would dart into the woods. With those thoughts still on my mind it picked up my scent and hurried off into the underbrush. As I had predicted Out of Africa was more than disappointed but we still had a lot of "moose" territory to cover and figured we would see another before reaching Katahdin.

We were continually amazed at the friendliness shown to us as thru-hikers when we were in town. We were following the trail along the road that lead us to Hanover, New Hampshire and were chatting about entering our 13th state, when a car approached from behind and came to a stop alongside us. The female driver rolled down her window and asked if we were thru-hikers, then invited us to her home if we were in need of a day off. Unfortunately we had just had a day off the previous day and as it was only late morning we thanked her for her gracious offer, but declined. Even when we weren't looking for it trail magic seemed to find us.

Now that we were in New Hampshire the White Mountains loomed larger than ever in our minds. The handbook quoted a thru-hiker saying "When you reach Hanover, you've done 80% of the miles, but you still have 50% of the work left." That's what concerned us, but at the same time was also intriguing. How could it possibly be any worse than what we had already done?

For weeks we had been discussing ways of lightening our packs when we picked up our winter gear in Glencliff, New Hampshire on August 24th. Out of Africa and I both decided that it would help us considerably if we could carry the absolute bare necessities (not that we weren't already), when we reached the White's and the tough ascents that would be facing us. Since we seemed to be staying mostly in the shelters, one of the tents was the most logical and heaviest article to go. Out of Africa's was lighter than mine so we agreed to mail mine home and we would share carrying hers. One of us would carry the tent, the other the poles and ground cloth. We still had vivid memories of Wayah Bald, but figured that if we did it once, we could do it again and hopefully wouldn't have to use it. We also decided to share a water filter, with Out of Africa keeping her filter cartridge and input hose in case of a malfunction, and utilizing mine. We also sent home simple things such as an extra pot gripper, the lid to Out of Africa's cook pot, one trowel, one water bag and our summer clothes with the exception of shorts. We were amazed at the difference in the weight of our packs by sharing these few items and would be glad we did once we reached the White's.

We were looking forward to reaching Glencliff and staying at Roger's House of Weather Hostel, which we had been hearing good things about, but much to our dismay found it closed when we arrived. We decided to re-supply and hike the one mile to Jeffers Brook Shelter, our first shelter in The White Mountain National Forest, and we were glad we did. It was one of those beautiful autumn New England days as we made our way up to the shelter. We arrived early in the afternoon and since we were unable to take a shower in town we decided to take advantage of no one being around and clean up in the stream in front of the shelter. The water already had an icy winter edge to it and as we poured it over our heads we got a brief headache the kind you get from eating ice cream too fast. Refreshed and somewhat cleaner we returned to the shelter for a relaxing afternoon. One by one our fellow hikers filed in and soon the shelter was full of familiar faces. We were all chatting excitedly about finally being in the White Mountains when a female hiker appeared whom we had not met yet and she greeted us with "How's it going?," her trademark hello. She was carrying an enormous pack and strapped to the back were three plastic chairs, the kind that children sit on. We knew immediately who she was as we had been reading her register entries for months as we were finally going to meet Skylark. A friend had given her <u>one</u> of the chairs so she would always have something to sit on when she stopped for a break on the trail. She was amazed at how sturdy it was and did in fact use it while resting. Unfortunately, early on in her hike, someone stole her pack and all of her belongings, including the chair. Undaunted by this misfortune, Skylark replaced her essential gear in order to continue her hike. <u>Three</u> of her thru-hiker friends (unbeknownst to the others) each bought her a new chair. Not wanting to choose which one to carry and risk offending one of her friends, she decided to carry <u>all three,</u> which she did, all the way to Katahdin!

Skylark was one of those individuals who you know you're going to like as soon as she opened her mouth to speak. She had the most positive attitude of anyone we had met so far on the trail and she loved to talk. You could feel the excitement in the air as we bedded down for the evening. We discussed our ascent the next day of Mount Moosilauke, our first 4,000 foot summit in the White's and although it would be a four mile climb, we were all looking forward to it. It was as if tomorrow was the first day of school as we all made our preparations and retired early. The next morning a rare thing happened. For the first time since we started our hike, EVERYONE was up at 5:30 a.m. Usually, we were the only ones up that early and we found it difficult to pack up quietly but did the best we could. What a welcome change of pace to be able to talk and make as much noise as we wanted. Everyone left at different times that morning but we would soon play hiker tag as the stronger hikers passed us, then we would pass them as they stopped for a break, until we reached what we thought was the summit. We looked off into the distance and saw a gradual climb to the treeless summit and were in awe as we covered the last mile to the top. Never in our lives had we witnessed such beauty and the higher we climbed the windier it became. We could also feel the temperature beginning to drop which would become the pattern for every mountain we would climb from here to Katahdin. Everyone gathered at the summit behind a pile of rocks someone had built to break the wind. We added another layer of clothing and took a break to discuss the climb as if we had just summited Mt. Everest. What a glorious feeling to sit atop our first peak in a mountain range we had been hearing about since Pennsylvania.

We both had a great deal of respect for these mountains and we would remember and repeat over and over again to ourselves, something Mr. Bean said to us the night before at Jeffers Brook Shelter. "How do you eat an elephant?," he asked. "Little bites at a time!" he laughed. From here on out, when we were faced with a daunting situation, we would remember, "Little bites of the elephant" to overcome our huge obstacles. The Whites can experience some of the worst weather in the lower 48 states. Temperatures can change quickly, which has resulted in many lives being lost. We had been told to adjust our mileage downward since the terrain is some of the most rugged we would experience on the A.T. We were comfortable (depending on the terrain) doing an average of 14-15 miles a day and had figured to decrease that to ten miles through the Whites. Little did we know exactly how rugged they were and ten miles would still be too many to attempt. Reluctantly we moved on to Beaver Brook Shelter where we stopped for lunch and had planned to stay for the night. We were on a real high and had too much energy to stop, so as we enjoyed the view into the Franconia Range, we decided to push on. It was difficult to enjoy the beauty of the brook we followed as we made our way down into Franconia Notch. This, by far, was the most difficult descent we would make and for 1.6 miles our knees screamed for mercy. The trail crews had helped as much as they possibly could by blasting away part of the boulders and placing wooden steps, but they were at an odd angle and were still tough to descend. Once we reached the bottom we had a hard time deciding whether to go on or stay. It was a nice spot for tenting, but we were feeling like super hikers and decided to go on and camp at Gordon Pond. We soon regretted our decision as we began to climb, and once again, we feared we were pushing ourselves over terrain that was extremely difficult. We reached the side trail to Gordon Pond and bushwhacked our way to the pond. It was a beautiful setting with an abundance of moose tracks around the area. Pond water was hard on our water filter so for the first time we had to boil water which is a slow, time consuming task. Our plan for not using the tent was short lived as we both piled into it, but it was to be a dry night and we were able to leave our packs hanging in a nearby tree. We were so tired we didn't care where we slept. This was to be one of our rare 12 mile days through the White Mountains.

We were feeling the effects, the next morning, from our first day in the White Mountains and our Mount Moosilauke weary legs were faced with climbing Kinsman Mountain. It was another one of those hand-over-hand climbs that went on forever and just when we thought we had reached the top we STILL had to climb North Kinsman Mountain. We were glad to reach Kinsman Pond Campsite and settled in for what appeared to be a quiet weekend with three weekenders being the only other occupants of the shelter. The clouds rolled in and proceeded to open up with a heavy downpour of rain and cooling wind. As we were preparing our evening meal, the caretaker arrived and announced that a party of ten weekenders would be arriving shortly and would be staying in the shelter. Before they would make it, however, six more hikers would come sliding in anxious to escape the rain. It is amazing how quickly the scene can change from peace and quiet to utter chaos as one by one the college group filed in, wet and tired. We had a front row seat as they dropped their packs and the contents went flying as they searched for dry, warm clothes. The entertainment continued as they prepared their group meal and our mouths watered as they sauteed vegetables (not frozen, but fresh) and rehydrated

The journey is more important than the destination

meat all to be piled on tortilla's topped with real cheese.   A near disaster sent everyone scrambling as it began to rain and a pot was knocked to the ground spilling its contents everywhere. We watched as they picked (most of it) up and placed it in a ziplock bag to be packed out. We would not have hesitated to eat what they had dropped (after a light washing) as we NEVER wasted food.   Our nerves were beginning to unravel as they tried to figure out how 20 people (plus gear), were going to fit into a shelter that at the most held 12 people. Somehow we all managed to squeeze together with bodies filling every available space and my journal entry reflected my mood. "Out of Africa and I are amazed that a week ago we were doing twice the miles in less time, that shows how difficult the Whites have been so far. The climb up Kinsman was unreal and probably the worst we've had. My nerves are on edge - too many people, too much rain, and I'm worried about the descent tomorrow." We slept very little and were eager to depart the next morning for North Woodstock to re-supply. The terrain was relatively easy after a slippery descent from the shelter and we were both anxious to see Lonesome Lake Hut, the first of seven huts we would pass while hiking in the Whites. The Appalachian Mountain Club operates these huts which provides lodging and meals. The huts are unique as they can only be reached by hiking to them. They are rather costly however, since all supplies must be packed in and out. Thru-hikers can often exchange work for staying in the huts and meals, but it is on a first-come first-served basis and as always, the early bird gets the worm. Lonesome Lake was spectacular but would go unrecorded on film as my camera battery decided to die, but luckily we were headed to town. I was a little too anxious to get there as I slipped crossing a wet log and my glasses took the blow as once again I fell to my knees. They were slightly bent and scratched and to my dismay would remain that way as the towns we would visit on the rest of our journey would not produce an Optician.

North Woodstock was filled with thru-hikers and since we had slept very little the night before, we opted for the comforts of an inexpensive motel room. A thru-hikers room was every mother's nightmare. Sleeping bags airing, wet ground cloths stretched from the shower rod, cooking pots and utensils soaking in the sink and dirty clothes "standing" by the door waiting to be laundered. After shopping for food, we would add flakes of instant mashed potatoes (compliments of Out of Africa), empty cardboard boxes, crumbs from our food bags, and dirt in general, from our gear. Our room could have easily been used for a vacuum cleaner salesman to demonstrate the power of their super deluxe model. We decided to mail food ahead to the post office at Mt. Washington to avoid carrying eight days worth of food through difficult terrain. We had very little time to shop, repackage it, and make it to the post office before closing time. It was time consuming enough to pack for five days, but this town visit we had to do it twice, and hope that it arrived at Mt. Washington before we did as there was no other place to re-supply until we reached Gorham in eight days.

August 28th found us departing North Woodstock and entering the Franconia Range which is mostly above treeline (about 4,000 feet in the Whites) and many consider this the most scenic section on the trail. We could have easily been at an amusement park as we roller coastered from one mountain to the next: Liberty Mountain, Little Haystack, Lincoln and Lafayette. We couldn't tell which one we were on and if we were actually at the summit or a false peak. The ascents and descents were not all that difficult, but they were (of course) rocky. A thick fog had shrouded the peaks the entire day, denying us any views. But, there was a different kind of beauty in the white clouds that surrounded us, and cloaked us in silence. I was feeling tired, but enjoying the hike despite the elements when a song came on my small radio that I had been hearing frequently. I turned and shouted to Out of Africa to change her radio station to mine and that I was dedicating the song to her. It was a song from a movie soundtrack and was sung by CeCe Winans and Whitney Houston. "Count on me through thick and thin; A friendship that will never end; When you are weak, I will be strong; Helping you to carry on; Call on me, I will be there; Don't be afraid; Please believe me when I say; Count on me." That pretty much said it all about Out of Africa's and my relationship as our journey of friendship continued to grow as we depended more and more on each other to tackle this rugged terrain. We arrived at Garfield Ridge Campsite and were glad to find a space in the shelter. The evenings were turning cooler and as I snuggled into my sleeping bag I entered in my journal: "WOW! Just when I think I've seen it all. Out of Africa and I continued to lighten our loads as we left our deodorant behind in town. It means more to have a light pack than to smell good." I closed my journal and gazed at the sky that had been dark with clouds all evening. As I turned out my flashlight, the moon, full and bright, suddenly appeared from behind a cloud and showed itself long enough for me to shake Out of Africa from the edge of sleep to see it, then just as quickly disappeared as if to say, "Goodnight."

My journal entries were beginning to sound the same every night and I could have easily written "Ditto." We had a difficult climb up South Mountain which was unbelievably steep. I turned and said to Out of Africa, "The closer we get to the top it's like I'm in a tunnel looking straight up, and all I can see are rocks and pines on both sides of the trail, and blue sky." The more we climbed that image never changed. We reached Zealand Falls Hut and decided to push on to Ethan Pond Campsite since the terrain looked to be flat, according to the maps. Flat it was. We covered the 4.5 miles to the shelter in two hours which was the same amount of miles we had just hiked, and had taken us all morning. Despite the hard days lately and wondering how much longer I could keep walking on my painful foot, I commented to Out of Africa that I keep seeing Katahdin and ridgewalking up to Mt. Washington in my mind and it keeps me going. All of the landmarks coming up between here and Maine I thought I could only dream about, were now only a couple hundred miles away.

We were entering the Presidential Range of mountains and it was a 25 mile section mostly above treeline. The maps looked like an erratic heartbeat that left our own hearts beating rapidly. Our handbook further quickened our pulse with the description of our first climb of the range, Webster Cliffs. "Allow some extra time for this section (which seemed to be what we did every day); if climbing and scrambling is not your thing (which it wasn't); tricky on windy, rainy days" (finally a plus for us, the sun was shining)! The cliffs weren't nearly as bad as expected. For 1 1/2 miles we would climb straight up, then level off, then climb and level off, and for the most part we enjoyed it as well as the views back to Crawford Notch. We stopped for lunch and stared out at the remaining peaks we would cross; Mt. Webster, Mt. Jackson, Mt. Pierce, Mt. Eisenhower, Mt. Franklin, and finally, the one and only, Mt. Washington. So many nights of dreaming of that mountain and there it was rising up in all its massive glory, surrounded by blue skies and sunshine. As the day progressed and we continued to reach higher elevations it gradually turned cooler and the wind increased considerably. We had planned to camp at Mitzpah Hut, but decided we would blow our budget and stay inside. What a treat. We threw our sleeping bags on one of the six bunks in our assigned room and curled up for a quick nap with visions of dinner dancing in our heads. Thru-hikers are never late for a meal when its prepared by someone else and our feet were under the table promptly at 6:00 p.m. Meals in the huts are served family style and our tastebuds danced with anticipation as bowls of beef stew, salad and broccoli were laid before us and a warm loaf of homemade bread set at the head of the table. We were beginning to notice that our manners were becoming nothing short of barbaric as we filled our plates and barely came up for air as we savored every bite. "It's as close to my mom's cooking as I'll get," I remarked to my weekend table mates, as they politely looked the other way. Out of Africa lost any trace of shyness as she volunteered to eat a young boy's pineapple cake that he neglected to save room for. Imagine, no room for dessert!

Much to our dismay we had to skip out on breakfast the next morning. We had 6.2 miles to cover to reach Mt. Washington and the post office before it closed. We were so excited to get up on the ridge that would lead us to Lake of the Clouds Hut and the summit of Mt. Washington, that we could have stayed for breakfast and a mid-morning snack as we easily covered the miles in 3 1/2 hours. I had been telling Out of Africa for weeks about how I use to dream of the ridgewalk to the hut and how I had kept a photo of it on my desk at work. I was also concerned about the changeable weather as the highest surface wind speed ever recorded was at the weather station atop Mt. Washington at 231 m.p.h. The "weather angels" were smiling down on us though, as they provided a beautiful, sunny day, albeit cold. The summit was like a magnet pulling me closer and closer and my feet barely touched the ground as I made my way over the rocky terrain burning film every step of the way. I rounded a curve in the trail and suddenly there it was, Lake of the Clouds Hut. I cried as I stood there gazing at it and realizing I was <u>really</u> there. For months I stared at that picture on my desk and would see myself me in the clouds, and now I could actually reach out and touch it. We took a short break before starting the 1 1/2 mile climb up the summit which sits at 6,288 feet in elevation. The wind during the climb would catch our packs and throw us off balance and it was so strong on top we could barely speak to each other and be heard. The weather was posted at 43 degrees with 45 m.p.h. winds and we were glad to escape them as we entered the Summit House which held the post office and a day room for use by hikers. We had to wait for the post office to open and we peeked through the window searching for our precious drop box and were greatly relieved to spot it on the bottom of the pile. We took a long break and visited with Buck-Buck while we filled our packs before leaving the comfort of the day room. We met Shaka outside as we were leaving, his kilt flapping in the wind, and he was finding it very difficult to walk and hold it down at the same time. The descent was like being on a freeway as it was crowded with day hikers since it was Labor Day weekend. We were ready to escape the masses of people and decided to push on to a campsite at Madison Springs Hut. The adrenalin rush of the morning soon left us as we gradually descended on the rocky trail that would take us to the hut at the base of Mt. Madison. When we arrived, we learned that the only tenting available was another 1/2 mile from the hut at Valley Way Campsite. The water source at the campsite was a spring, so we decided to fill our bottles and water bag before leaving the hut. Our weary legs revolted as we descended steeply to the campsite carrying our newly resupplied packs, as well as a full water bag. As is common in the Whites, the tentsites are all on platforms which is fine as long as you are carrying a free standing tent, which we were not. It was getting late and we were not in the mood to search out another tent site and decided we would simply sleep under the stars on top of one of the platforms. With that decided we set about preparing dinner when a group of four weekend hikers arrived. They WERE carrying free-standing tents and thought we could all fit on the platform together as they are quite large, but instead helped us to clear an area where we could pitch Out of

Africa's tent where we soon collapsed. My journal entry for the night reflected: "Less than a month and we should be at Katahdin and on our way home." Home was sounding better all the time.

It was always difficult to pack up and head out in the morning when we were faced with a climb back to the trail, and to also know that there was a boulder strewn mountain waiting for us, made it less than inviting. We both had a sleepless night as our knees ached from the previous day's descents, and neither of us were in a positive state of mind as we hoisted our packs onto our backs. Our legs were stiff, and our feet sore, as we made our way up the rocks to the summit. The descent would leave us screaming for mercy as we had reached our limit of pain. We took turns shedding tears as we made our way down Mt. Madison. Tears of frustration and pain. It seemed that the rocks would never end and at one rest stop I told Out of Africa that it would be easier to just throw myself off the rocks. I would make it down a lot quicker and it couldn't possibly be more painful than the agony we were enduring by picking our way over these huge jagged boulders. I had developed new blisters from yesterday's hike and every step was painful. My confidence on the rocks was non-existent and once again my decision-making process was slow and confused. It took us all morning to go 3.8 miles and we wondered if we could make it the four miles to Pinkham Notch where we hoped to camp for the night. Our lunch break was quiet as we both were hurting and were trying to psyche ourselves up to make it to the notch. The terrain improved as we left our peaceful spot by a stream and we made good time to Pinkham Notch Camp, a full service lodge run by the Appalachian Mountain Club. We were greeted by members of our hiker family and it was obvious to them that we were both physically and mentally burned out. We discussed our options of staying at the lodge, pushing on and camping, or hitching into Gorham early instead of in two more days as we originally planned after covering the additional 21 miles. We spoke with Shaka, Quiet Man and McCoy, and it was as if we were wanting them to tell us to go to town for some much needed rest for our weary bodies, and peace of mind for our souls. We finally convinced ourselves that we needed the comforts of town and put our thumbs out for someone to whisk us away. We soon arrived at Hiker's

Paradise in Gorham, New Hampshire, which was one of the finest hostels we stayed in. Bruno and Mary Ann Janicki more than provided the comfort we needed in their hostel and as Out of Africa showered I wrote in my journal: "I just want to be out of New Hampshire and in Maine. Never did I dream it would be so tough, but we've finally learned to get off the trail when we feel this bad - sleep in tomorrow and pancakes for breakfast."

We ended up spending two nights in Gorham. We arrived on Sunday afternoon, and the post office was closed on Monday in observance of Labor Day and since Gorham was a planned maildrop for Midnite we had no choice but to stay the extra night. We were anxious to reach Katahdin, still 320 miles away, but in our present state, the rest was needed to get us there. The hostel was full of thru-hikers as once again we (and everyone else) were taking cover to wait out Hurricane Edouard. Midnite said it reminded her of the slumber parties she had as a child. Everyone staying up late talking or watching T.V., and eating all their favorite snacks. The camaraderie among us is more than just a familiar face trying to reach a common goal, but, the lending of a helping hand when the going gets tough. There were plenty of hands at the hostel to help pick us up, and get us back on track mentally for the rest of the journey, or at least to get us over Wildcat Mountain, the next obstacle in our path. Our time off in Gorham was enjoyable and Out of Africa discovered another American delicacy, Dunkin Donuts. She was like a kid in a candy store as she eyed every single donut trying to make her decision as to which one would make her tummy happy, and since there were so many to choose from, we returned the next day to taste test a few more. Unfortunately, our rest and relaxation was clouded with the thought of tackling Wildcat Mountain when we returned to the trail. It was to be another steep rock climb and we discussed it and the hold it seemed to have over us. We left Gorham early in the afternoon in hopes that Midnite could have her glasses fixed in the morning, but the Optician was closed. "It would have been nice to have alleviated one pain," Midnite said as we left town. We felt rested but were dragging our feet as we returned to Pinkham Notch Camp. We decided to camp at the base of Wildcat Mountain and tackle it first thing the next morning. We spent the evening stretched out in Out of Africa's tent talking about the obstacles we had overcome in the last five months, and we realized that we were dwelling too much on the negatives and not looking at the positives. Granted, we were both anxious to get to Katahdin, but we were looking at the future and not living in the present, despite how tough the days were. We both agreed that we were tired and hurting, but this was the last leg of our journey and from what we had heard, the best was yet to come. We were so close, but yet so far away, so the daily showers and wearing clean clothes could wait another few weeks. We had put too much into this and dreamed too long to turn it into work when it should be the best part of our trip. Wildcat Mountain would turn out to be not nearly as tough as we had built it up to be, and we did a short day of six miles to Carter Notch Hut. Midnite discovered during a break that her hipbelt had cracked and discussed with Quiet Man at the hut whether to try and order a replacement or "limp" the rest of the way with it broken. She hadn't noticed it feeling any different and thought she could get by. Quiet Man felt she should have it replaced and offered to call Gregory (the maker of her pack) and order the part for her as he would be in town before we were and have it shipped to Andover, Maine, our next re-supply stop.

Our handbook informed us that "the toughest section on the Trail for many thru-hikers was from Gorham to Stratton (Maine)" and that would turn out to be an understatement. It continued to read, "If it is rainy, you will be slowed down even more by muddy areas, wet roots, and slippery rocks." The descents would find us sliding on our backsides with no footholds or even roots to grab on to. We were getting quite good at grabbing a small sapling, swinging around it and going down the rocks backwards, as it was the only way down. My nightly journal entries were beginning to sound the same every night. "The terrain, doing miles and getting done are beginning to get to me. We can't push miles over this terrain, but that feeling of wanting to finish and stop hurting is also there. I try to think - relax and enjoy it, but if we do short days it will take longer. I'm tired of the food, being dirty and hurting, but then I always feel this way when I'm tired." Out of Africa and I frequently talked about being home. We said we were going to wear white every single day and I was being driven crazy by an advertisement on the radio for pineapple/orange yogurt, which I vowed to eat a gallon of when I got home. Our fellow thru-hikers were feeling the same as we were, everyone wanted to be finished and go home, but we still had miles to go.

Lindi: *We always seem to be talking about Midnite falling and hurting herself. Maybe people are thinking, "Didn't the other one fall?"   Well, yes I did - several times.   I fell four times and cut my knee in exactly the same place and now have a permanent scar.   I was always tripping over something, and sometimes I lagged so far behind I thought Midnite had gone home and left me.   But, she was always there in the end - waiting for me.*

CHAPTER 7

MAINE, "THE WAY LIFE SHOULD BE"

Gentian Pond Campsite was to be our last shelter in New Hampshire. We had been hiking the last few days with Lemstar, Gearmaster, and Merlin and we were all looking forward to crossing into our 14th and final state, Maine. After an uneventful five miles the sign marking the state line came into view and the tears began to flow. We had been saying for weeks that if we could just make it to Maine, we would be able to deal with the physical pain because our mental state of mind would greatly improve knowing we were at least in the same state as Mt. Katahdin. We were two happy campers as we stared at the sign that said "Welcome to Maine, The Way Life Should Be" and "282.7 miles left to go." We certainly hoped that was going to be true. The White Mountains was the way life shouldn't be!

Our welcome mat to Maine was Goose Mountain. A sheer slab of rock that descended 40-50 yards with not so much as a crack in it to help us down. We sort of sat down on the rock with our knees tucked up under our chin and inched our way slowly down the face of it. Our knees were so beat up from the rigors of the Whites that we were afraid they would never straighten out once we reached the bottom. We were continuing to keep our daily mileage low because even though we were out of the White Mountains, the terrain had not improved, and wouldn't until we reached Stratton.

Mahoosuc Notch. The mere mention of the name would stand our hair on end. It is the toughest mile on the A.T., and it isn't even a climb. We had been hearing about these massive jumble of rocks for weeks and now we were about to face them head on. This mile long section consists of thousands of boulders, some the size of small houses, that have broken off the steep slopes of the surrounding peaks. These slopes are so high and steep that they block out all direct sunlight

The stars exist that we might know how high our dreams can soar

and ice can be found in the notch all year. There had been a threat of rain the night before and Midnite's "Connecticut ankle" had been feeling weak. Taping it with duct tape gave her a little extra support over the wet rocks. The sky was dark as we gathered ourselves to enter this mile long section of trail who's reputation was as notorious as the Whites. Our handbook quoted a thru-hiker advising to "Treat it like a jungle gym." It had been many years since I had played on a jungle gym and I certainly wasn't wearing a 40 pound pack at the time, but Out of Africa and I were positive and vowed to take it slow and enjoy it as much as we could. It was as difficult as we expected but it wasn't any worse than what we had already done over the last five months. We started down into the notch, following the white blazes deeper into the stone maze. Crawling under rocks balanced on top of each other to form a tunnel, we pushed and pulled ourselves, and each other over rocks with no visible hand or foot holds. We were like flies clinging to the slick rocks. "How did you get there?" Midnite called, standing in the shade of a house size boulder. "Put your foot there, and here's a hand hold," Out of Africa said. Sometimes, the rocks were sharp and bruised our knees and hands, and tore at our nails. Was it over time, or a sudden upheaval that sent these huge boulders crashing into the notch, we wondered, as two hours later we emerged at the end, finally reaching an area to rest, and take our packs off. We had conquered the notch, but our day was far from over as we still had to tackle Mahoosuc Arm which was steep and it had begun to rain. We began to push ourselves to make it to the top before it rained too hard and the footing became treacherous. Our hands grabbed at every available tree root to help pull our weakened legs up to the top. Just as we were about to reach the summit, my foot slipped off of a rock and I shouted to Out of Africa, "My ankle's gone again!" Memories of Connecticut came flooding back as we found a spot out of the wind to stop for lunch. The temperature was dropping rapidly and I was cooling off fast after our climb, but I really didn't care. We huddled together shoving food in our mouths to provide some warmth and energy before pushing on to Speck Pond Campsite. I really didn't know if my ankle would carry me to the shelter let alone the additional seven miles we had planned to Baldpate Lean-To where we hoped to stay for the night. The rain continued and the fog rolled in as we set out for Speck Pond and a few minutes later, Out of

Africa slipped on a wet log and turned her knee. The situation had gone from bad to worse and we both just wanted to sit down and cry, but instead, gathered ourselves as best we could, picked up our hiking sticks, and limped to the shelter. No matter how hard we tried to keep our spirits up and enjoy the rest of our journey, we continually had obstacles such as this thrown in our path and at this stage of the game all we could think about was hanging on until we reached Katahdin. Our bodies were feeling the rigors of hiking over 1,800 miles and that brought us down psychologically. We knew we could hike no further this day and settled in at the shelter for a long afternoon of being curled up in our sleeping bags and listening to our radios to keep our minds occupied. One by one, Gearmaster, Lemstar, and Merlin filed in and we sat around drinking hot chocolate and relating our experiences through the notch. Gearmaster was unbelievable. A thin, but strong hiker, he was ready to turn around and do it again. We marvelled at his strength and positive attitude as we were feeling as if we had just left Springer Mountain and hadn't developed our hiker legs yet.

As the day progressed, we decided it would be best if we hiked the 4.5 miles to Grafton Notch the next day and rest our injuries in Andover. The roads in Maine are not well traveled and we were worried about hitching a ride into town. We had planned to stay at the Pine Ellis Bed and Breakfast when we arrived and knew that they provided a shuttle from the trail, so we asked a weekend hiker, who was on his way back to town, if he would try to arrange for someone to pick us up the next morning. He was happy to help us out, but we had no guarantee that there would be anyone waiting for us when we arrived, but it was a risk we needed to take.

The next morning dawned with no change in the weather and we were both concerned about the climb up Old Speck Mountain over more wet rocks. Midnite's ankle was still painful and often gave out on her. Some months ago, Out of Africa's knees had begun to ache, and now they were creaking as she climbed and sounded as they needed a good oiling. We were in hopes of arranging a day or two of slackpacking from Andover to give them both a break from the weight of our packs; that is, if we made it there. We arrived at the parking lot sooner than we anticipated as Old Speck didn't turn out to be as difficult as we had expected. We anxiously watched motorists pass us by as we pulled up a rock to wait, we hoped, for our ride to town. It wasn't long before a car pulled into the lot and Paul Trainor, the owner of the B&B, jumped out and greeted us with a handshake, hot coffee, and apples.

We could not have asked for more accommodating hosts in Paul and Ilene Trainor. They went to great extremes to make us feel welcome and comfortable in their home and were more than happy to arrange shuttles for us so we could rest our bodies and still cover some miles by slackpacking for two days. I phoned home, as I always did as soon as we made it to town, and I relayed to Out of Africa my mother's comment that "The days were dragging" until they were to meet us in Millinocket, Maine to bring us home. I whole heartedly agreed.

September 10th blessed us with sunshine and a ten mile slackpack day. After fueling our bodies with a breakfast of french toast, sausage, fresh fruit, and pastry, lovingly prepared by Ilene and Paul, we were taxied to the trail. It felt so good to hike without our packs, but it took awhile to get use to the "light" feeling and we felt off balance without the weight on our backs. Mid-afternoon brought the rains again, but it didn't phase us in the least. It was a treat to climb without fear of falling, and to know that we would be returning to the B&B that evening for warm showers and dry clothes. After a brief wait, Paul arrived, this time bringing us iced tea to drink as he chauffeured us back to the B&B. Midnite's ankle still felt weak despite not carrying her pack, but we both hoped that another day of slacking would make a difference. We arranged to hike the next day 13.4 miles to a road and meet Ilene with our packs. It was another beautiful day as we crossed Bemis Mountain with hopes of catching our first glimpse of Katahdin. There were so many mountain ranges that we couldn't tell which one was Katahdin, so we can only assume that we saw it. It was so enjoyable to walk along the top of the ridge looking down at the blue waters of Long Lake. Ilene arrived shortly after we did and treated us to more iced tea and cherry tomatoes from their garden. After farewells were said, we decided to cook an early dinner and hike another 3.7 miles to Sabbath

Pond Lean-To, giving us a 17 mile day. Our packs felt as if they weighed a ton after skipping along for two days with nothing more than a fanny pack. Midnite's new hipbelt arrived during our stay in Andover and as she was replacing the old one she noticed a crack in the other side of the belt so it was a good thing that she listened to Quiet Man and ordered the part. Light was fading as we arrived at the lean-to and was greeted by Skylark whom we hadn't seen since Lake of the Clouds Hut. Skylark was always a joy to be around. No matter what the conditions were, she was always cheerful and positive, and a positive mind was what we were in need of these days. What a treat to have the shelter all to ourselves - sort of like a girls night out.

Five minutes out of the shelter the next morning, it started raining again. The cooler fall temperatures made it most miserable to hike in and we were always looking for something to brighten our day. As I approached a small incline in the trail I heard a snort, like a deer, to the left of me. I stopped immediately and turned to see where Out of Africa was. She was no where in sight and I could not detect any movement in the underbrush, so I continued on assuming it was a deer. An hour later I again heard a snorting sound, but this time I could see the huge rack of a moose. I froze and silently spoke to Out of Africa to hurry or she would miss it. She was soon on my heels and knew I was looking at something since I seldom stopped in the middle of the trail unless to take a break. I motioned for her to look next to a tree and we were amazed at the size of the rack on this bull and whispered that he must be enormous. With that said, he STOOD up and as we were catching our breath from witnessing this sight, another, equally as big, bull stood up next to him. What good fortune we had to not only see one, but two and were still talking about them when we stopped for lunch. The moment we dropped our packs, two Canadian Jays flew into the tree next to us and decided to join us for lunch. They were quite bold and came within inches of us as we ate. They would sit and watch us, although they refused the crumbs we offered them (smart birds - we didn't like what we were having either), then would fly up into the tree above us and watch us from that vantage point for awhile. They were beautiful birds and we would enjoy seeing them frequently, in higher altitudes, throughout Maine. It continued to rain off and on the remainder of the day and we were beginning to tire of having wet socks and boots, flashbacks to the spring rains in Virginia. Rain on the trail is one of those good and bad elements to contend with. Its good for keeping the springs running and therefore we never had a shortage of water, but it also produced the hordes of mosquitoes we had to contend with in Connecticut and Massachusetts. Of course, no rain means no pesty bugs, but also a shortage of water, so its just one of those things you just accept, since you can't change it anyway. Once again, Skylark joined us at Piazza Rock Lean-To and we discussed the next day's hike, as we huddled around a small fire. It looked to be a real knee burner, with still the threat of more rain. We were optimistic about the hike and determined not to dwell on the difficulty and just take it as it came.

September 13th was my 37th birthday and Out of Africa presented me with a homemade card (but no cake, wonder why?), before we set off in a drizzle for our first climb of the day, Saddleback Mountain. Despite the cooler temperatures we were still hiking in shorts and sport bras under our rain jackets. We stopped for a break before we began our climb and discussed whether to take our jackets off as we always warmed up no matter what the weather. We decided to leave them on which was a very intelligent decision on our part since the summit was above treeline and as each step brought us closer to the top, the wind increased and the temperature fell. It was, at least, level on top and we crossed as fast as we could, first of all to keep warm, and second to get below treeline as fast as possible. The wind was so strong that neither of us wanted to stop for a break, but I was always on the lookout for signs of hypothermia and knew we needed to be eating and drinking to keep our body temperature from dropping below normal. The trail dropped between some large rocks and we quickly took off our packs and inhaled a snack and soon were on our way again. I expressed concern for Skylark who was hiking alone in this bad weather, but as we began our climb up The Horn, she appeared through the fog, a smile on her face, and exclaimed, "Isn't this awesome." It was indeed, but we weren't smiling like she was. The wind at the summit of The Horn was worse than at the top of Saddleback Mountain and with one more climb to make, Saddleback Junior, our optimism went flying with the wind. Not being able to see two feet in front of us, and being cold and wet, produced one thought: get below treeline, no matter what the cost. We would slide, jump, anything we needed to, to descend the rocks to make it back to the protection of the trees. Once again we were a pitiful lot as we stopped for lunch and added an extra layer of clothing to our chilled bodies. What a way to spend a birthday and my birthday photo I posed for at the lean-to, pretty much said it all. Blood running down my leg from my knee, my hair and clothes dripping wet, but, there was a smile on my face, probably from Out of Africa's promise of Little Debbie's and Mountain Dew when we reached Stratton in a few days. I had written in my journal, "When I was planning this trip, I had visions of spending my birthday stretched out on a rock, next to a pond, soaking up the sun. It couldn't have been further from that image!" I had been saving one of my mom's inspirational sayings for my birthday. It appeared to be lengthy as it was on a larger piece of paper than usual, and it was certainly appropriate. It read:

For me the hills, no winding valley ways, Hemming me in and sheltering my days; For me the effort, the vast, far flung goal, Great draughts of beauty for my thirsting soul. From far above, the mists that drift below drown in soft azure beauty, sin and woe, and oh the joy of conquest, looking back to say, "My feet are bruised, but I have climbed today."

After a cold, windy and rainy night, we again departed the shelter in a drizzle that soon turned into an all-out rain. We had discussed with Skylark the night before where she would be heading today and her goal was the Summit House on Sugarloaf Mountain. The Summit House was an enclosed building with electricity and a wood stove and the thought of warming ourselves and drying our clothes was the only thing that kept us going throughout the day. We really had our rain pace working as we only took one break in the morning and pushed on to Spaulding Lean-To so we would at least be out of the rain for lunch. We didn't bother to put on dry clothing while we ate since it would only become soaked as soon as we left the shelter. We quickly ate and set off again with a warm fire firmly planted in our minds. We passed a southbounder who informed us that there was already a group of hikers at the Summit House and they had a nice fire going when he left, which is exactly what we wanted to hear. We reached the side trail that would lead us the 1/2 mile to the summit of Sugarloaf Mountain and it looked as if a dam had been opened. The trail was literally running ankle deep in water. We began the steep climb up not even attempting to stay out of the pouring water since our boots were already saturated. We finally reached the top only to be unable to locate the building as everything was surrounded by a thick fog. Luckily the southbounder had told us that it sat to the left of the trail and we eventually ran into it. How very happy we were to be there. We quickly peeled off our wet clothing and started pulling our gear out to set next to the fire to dry. We were told by the other hikers that all the rain was leftover from yet another hurricane and that the weather would hang around for a few more days. Despite the lousy weather, we couldn't help notice the beauty of the turning leaves as they were scattered about the trail. Fall was definitely upon us. It wasn't long before the door opened and in walked Skylark, drenched of course, but grinning from ear to ear and exclaiming, as she always did, "This place is awesome." It was quite cozy to be in an enclosed shelter and watch the thick fog swirling around in the high winds and listening to the rain pelt the glass. We revelled in the fact that at this point we had less than 200 miles left to Katahdin.

The next morning, the fog had lifted and it wasn't raining, at least for the moment. We were on our way to Stratton for hot showers and another re-supply. Our knees ached continually but we had reached the point of just living with it. Ibuprofen (the drug of choice on the trail), no longer helped to alleviate the pain and discomfort, but we continued to take it anyway. We both agreed that we were anxious to finish so that we could quit living in pain. Neither of us really wanted our journey to be over, and had we not been plagued by these aches our dispositions would have been better than they were. Many sleepless nights had us thinking more and more about going home. The thoughts of "What will we do when we're finished" were beginning to creep into our minds. This was something neither of us wanted to think about.

Out of Africa was really puzzled by a sign she had been seeing at road crossings. It showed a moose with the letter

"X" and then "ING" under the silhouette. She thought of many explanations for the sign, but could only come up with - Moose "X"ing. It seemed so simple after Midnite explained to her that it was Moose <u>Crossing</u>. Ding!

We departed Stratton on September 18th and although it wasn't raining when we left town, it started as soon as our feet touched the trail. The one thing that would keep us from going insane from the incessant rain and foggy conditions, was that each day brought us one day closer to seeing the mountain of our dreams. We were hoping that since we left Stratton that (as we had been told) the tough terrain would become easier, but that was not the case as we climbed to Myron A. Avery Campsite. We were glad that we were staying there for the night as the shelter was going to be torn down sometime in 1997 and we were given a little history of the hikers who had stayed there before us by the caretakers Susan and Tom. We located them in the caretaker's cabin a few yards from the shelter and were quite envious of their accommodations. It was a small, cozy cabin filled with books and best of all a fire. They invited us in for a chat and we were thrilled to see the trail register that Grandma Gatewood signed on September 4, 1964. This was also the cabin Bill Irwin had been forced to stay in for three days as he waited out a snowstorm. How happy we were to be there. Susan and Tom brought leftover beans and bread to the shelter for us. The beans went well with Out of Africa's instant mashed potatoes. They stayed and chatted for a while, pointing out two snowshoe hares foraging behind the shelter. The hares are well named with their huge hind feet. Their fur was still mostly brown, but in a few weeks, it would turn white. It had stopped raining, but the freezing fog still lingered, dripping from the trees, leaving us damp and cold. We could hear the Canadian Jays calling, and soon they appeared, flying closer, watching as Tom put crumbs in his hand and held it out. One of the jays flew down, perched on Tom's hand, and ate the crumbs before flying off. They are large, bold birds, sometimes called "camp robbers." They were gone before Midnite had a chance to get her camera. She did manage, however, to take a photograph of a spruce grouse, also called "fool hens," because they apparently have no fear of people. This one stayed on its perch while she photographed it, looking at us over it's shoulder. At other times, they had exploded from the undergrowth, running ahead of us up the trail. It was beginning to get dark now, and Susan and Tom wished us sweet dreams before retiring to their cabin. We had little else to do after dinner these days except climb into our sleeping bags to stay warm and we were usually asleep by 7:30 p.m., dreaming of fuzzy slippers and roaring fires.

Our next stop for the night was West Carry Pond Lean-To. I slipped off a log bog bridge on the way there, and spent such a long time getting up that I missed a moose that Midnite saw. It ambled out of the bushes beside the pond, saw Midnite, and took off down the trail. West Carry Pond Lean-To is in a beautiful setting, with tall trees, a view of the water, and plenty of logs to sit on. I awoke sometime during the night. It was pitch black, and I could hear strange noises. It was the loons calling. There seemed to be dozens of them. One would start, and the other would take it up. It was an eerie, faraway sound. The essence of Maine. It went on long into the night. I tried to wake Midnite so she could share it with me, but she mumbled something, and went on sleeping. Warm in my sleeping bag, surrounded by the dark night, I listened to the loons calling to each other.

At last, the terrain was improving and we easily covered the ten miles to Pierce Pond by lunchtime. We were beginning to feel like our old selves again. Finally a day without rain but we were about to realize where all the rain went, besides in our boots. We left Pierce Pond and were anxious to hike to the Kennebec River but first we had to cross the dam at the edge of the pond. Sounded simple enough, but the rain had flooded everything and the only way to cross was on a log (wet of course), with the water rushing under it and on either side. Out of Africa could see the fear in my eyes and volunteered to take the lead and made it safely across. I started to cross, but stopped and went back, all the while listening to my partner shout encouragement to me. There was no other way around it so I started again and this time made it half way before my legs started going weak on me. I stopped, said a quick prayer for God's guidance and continued and soon joined Out of Africa safely on the other side. I quickly realized that I was going to need all the help I could get crossing these rain swollen streams, but I had two great partners, Out of Africa and God on my side. We followed Pierce Pond Stream as we gradually descended towards the Kennebec River, and were in awe of the strength and power of the water as it rushed beside us. After a few more tricky crossings, the Kennebec River finally came into view. Words cannot describe the feeling I had as I looked down at it. "This river," according to our handbook "was to be our last major obstacle to delay us from reaching Katahdin." This is an extremely dangerous crossing and it is highly recommended not to attempt to ford it. A thru-hiker lost his life here in 1985 while attempting a ford when the dam located upstream released its water. This is done automatically and not on any set schedule so it's never known when the water level will rise. Because of this unfortunate incident, a ferry service was put into operation to allow for a safe crossing. We reached the shoreline of the river and retrieved the orange signal flag that alerts the ferry that a hiker is waiting to cross. Between the hours of 10:00 a.m. and noon, and 3:00 p.m. and 5:00 p.m. the ferry will make its way across the river. After our packs were safely placed inside the canoe, Steve (the captain of our ship) instructed us on how we would return to the opposite shore. Midnite agreed to help paddle us across and was amazed how strong the current was. We would first paddle upstream, then battle our way to the middle of the river and at the moment Steve instructed, we would pull in our oars and drift down to the shore. It had been a pretty exciting day as it was becoming clearer to us just exactly how close we were to Katahdin after our crossing of the Kennebec. The fact that we had hiked over 2,000 miles reinforced that our journey was quickly drawing to an end.

We finally had a break in the weather and the gray, drab skies gave way to glorious sunshine. We were basking in its warmth next to Moxie Pond when we were rewarded with our first sighting of a loon. Or at least we think we saw one. It disappeared as suddenly as it appeared and Midnite stood poised with her camera aimed at the spot where it had been. After several minutes, she gave up and returned her camera to her hip pouch thinking that it must have surfaced somewhere else. We began to put our packs on and suddenly it appeared again. Midnite reached for her camera and then

Nothing is ever too hard to do if your faith is strong and your purpose is true. So never give up and never stop, just journey on to the mountaintop.

it was gone. We would have liked to have stayed and played hide and seek a while longer, but we figured it must be camera shy and departed without its photograph. We were joking about the double cable crossing at the edge of the pond that some (daring) thru-hikers use to cross Baker Stream. The cables were placed across the stream to allow power workers to cross. There was one cable for your hands, and one below it for your feet. "Who," I commented to Out of Africa, "would be crazy enough to cross on them." We walked a few hundred yards along a dirt road and then followed the trail to the stream. The water was a nightmare: waist deep and the current was strong, with nothing but submerged rocks to aid in crossing it.

Mel: *Out of Africa knew what I was going to say before I began to speak: "I can't do it," but this time she agreed that it would be a tricky ford. "I'm going back to the cables and cross them" I told her. They suddenly didn't seem quite so ridiculous and as far as I was concerned, had to be safer than the cold, rain swollen stream. Upon reaching the cables I didn't hesitate, but climbed the crude ladder and started to inch my way across, my arms stretched over my head. I looked across to the other side and estimated it was about 30 yards before I would have solid ground under my feet again, and glanced only once at the water five feet below my feet. All was going better than I expected until I reached the halfway point. My arms began to tire and my legs started to quiver, and I could feel the strain on my back as my pack was pulling me backwards. I knew if I stopped I would have a hard time getting my momentum going again as the cables were beginning to go up to reach the ladder on the opposite side. I pushed myself on to finish before I lost my grip. Safely back on solid ground I shouted to Out of Africa, "Take your time and you'll do just fine." She climbed to the cables but was unable to reach the top cable. Relieved, she shouted across that she was going back to the original crossing. "I'll bushwhack my way to the trail and help you across," I told her. A sense of panic filled me as I realized that Out of Africa was on one side and I was on another. There was no way for her to reach me without fording the stream. What if she couldn't make it? I suddenly felt as if we were back in Connecticut again and she would turn her back and walk away from me. I quickly fought my way through the thick underbrush and made it back to the trail* *just in time to see Out of Africa come racing up the trail towards me. "How did you get here," I asked, amazed to see her so soon.*

Lindi: *I couldn't believe that Midnite was actually serious about crossing Baker Stream on the cables. I wanted to talk her out of it, because, I really didn't want to do it. She was never happy crossing on rocks, but this looked twice as bad to me. I watched silently as Midnite climbed to the wires, and started across, her arms and legs extended, her backpack pulling her backwards. "What do I do," I thought, "if she falls in?" The water was deep and dark brown, flowing swiftly. What would I tell her mother? What about her camera? How could we dry everything out? It's funny what thoughts went through my head. While I was still thinking, she was across, and it was my turn. I was relieved when I couldn't reach the top wire! I went back to the first crossing. I hesitated for a few seconds. It's now or never, I thought. Crossing over water on rocks, doesn't bother me, but the water here was swift, and deep. Quickly, before I could think about it, I stepped to the first rock, and then just kept going, hopping from rock to rock. I slipped off once, my right boot filled with water, and then I was across. I saw Midnite coming through the bushes towards me. "How did you get here?" she said, almost indignantly. "On the rocks," I proudly told her.*

It was good to both be on the same side again. We found a nice spot, dropped our packs, and lit a cigarette!

Later in the day we met a southbounder who informed us that the fords would only get worse. I was really becoming concerned and wrote in my journal, "I hope the good Lord gets us across the fords tomorrow. I have to wonder what else can be put in front of us to test us. Just when we thought we had seen and done it all: rock climbing, Mahoosuc Notch, hiking above treeline in a storm, the White Mountains, the thick fog on White Top Mountain in Virginia, swollen streams, What else? Oh yeah, KATAHDIN." Out of Africa and I had made a bet that our boots would not be dry until we reached Millinocket, the first town after Katahdin. I said they wouldn't dry out, and she said they would. A Little Debbie and Mountain Dew was riding on it.

Our knees were still bothering us. They would become stiff at lunch and we hated to sit down for any length of time because it took them so long to stretch out again. Despite our continuing aches and pains, we were enjoying the pageantry of colors that fall was painting on the leaves as they were changing, it seemed, right before our eyes. Ah yes, Maine, The Way Life Should Be!

Looking at the map for our hike on September 20th it revealed the last climb, of any size, between here and Katahdin. Moxie Bald was worth the steep climb as the top afforded us great views. The descent was gradual and the scenery just as rewarding as what we had witnessed on top. The southbounder we had met who warned us of difficult fords was not exaggerating as we approached the outlet to Bald Mountain Pond. The water was swift and our only means of crossing was on two logs that were jammed next to each other end to end, then rock hopping on submerged rocks. We combed the bank and each found an extra hiking stick to help us keep our balance as we tight rope walked the slippery logs. Unshaken (and luckily dry) we cruised along the trail next to Bald Mountain Stream until it met the West Branch of the Piscataquis River. We surveyed the situation noticing that both bodies of water had exceeded their banks by 10-15 feet as a result of the endless days of rain. Since this was to be our widest and deepest ford, we decided to remove our socks, but leave our boots on to help keep our balance. The icy water reached the tops of our thighs by mid-stream and the current increased speed the further we went. Safely reaching the other side we didn't hesitate and began the more shallow and calmer ford of the Piscataquis River. This being our first formidable ford, we felt very proud of ourselves, as we did everytime we overcame a fear or obstacle on our journey, and although we never realized it at the time, each hurdle we cleared continued to build our confidence. Despite our saturated, heavy boots, the three miles to Horseshoe Canyon Lean-To were magnificent. The trail hugged the banks of the river as it cut its way through the canyon while the opposite shore met a sheer wall of rock. Once again we were impressed by the strength of the river as its power increased as it descended over rocks creating small waterfalls. I commented to Out of Africa, "Maine is really showing its stuff today." The sounds of the river lulled us to sleep that night as we dreamed of hiking into Monson the next day - Midnite's last maildrop and our final re-supply of the trip.

After an easy and uneventful ford of the East Branch of the Piscataquis River we reached Shaw's Boarding House in Monson. This hostel is a legend along the trail and Keith and Pat Shaw, according to our handbook, "Have welcomed more than 18,000 hikers into their home." I had seen so many photographs of the hostel, with thru-hikers posing in front of the house next to the large wooden cut-out hiker with the words "Welcome" painted on it. And welcome we were! The Shaw's provide AYCE (All You Can Eat) meals served family style and our mouths were watering for breakfast the next morning as soon as we arrived. After settling into our comfortable room, we began, for the last time, our "town" chores. The first stop was the post office for Midnite's drop box and mail. When we entered the post office we immediately recognized McCoy with her trademark ball hat which she always wore backwards. We last saw her in Gorham, New Hampshire and we chatted about the fords and the fact that we only had 114 miles left to go. As Midnite requested her box, the post mistress exclaimed, "So you're Melody Blaney. It's about time you got here, I was running out of room to store your mail." "What do you mean," Midnite asked bewildered. It seems that Midnite's hometown newspaper had reported our progress, as they had been doing periodically during our trek, and mentioned that she would be spending her birthday on the trail and it would be nice if she would receive a card or note at her last maildrop in Monson. Midnite's eyes grew large as the post mistress handed her a bundle of over 75 cards and letters, the most that had ever been sent to a thru-hiker in Monson. Skylark and McCoy were sitting in front of the hostel as we returned from the post office and upon seeing Midnite's "haul" commented that they hadn't received that much mail the entire time they had been on the trail, and proceeded to give Midnite a hard time, all in fun, of course. She was deeply touched that so many people from home had taken time away from their busy lives to send her wishes for her birthday, as well as encouraging words and prayers. Over the last 5 1/2 months, Midnite was pleasantly surprised at each maildrop to find cards and letters from people she had never met, but who followed our hike. It was with delight that Midnite sorted out her last, larger than usual, maildrop and commented to Out of Africa that she was so glad that this was the final one. We joked a number of times throughout the day that "This will be the last time we have to do this or that task, and the next town we'll be in will be Millinocket." The adrenalin and excitement was beginning to build for the final leg of our journey, the 100 Mile Wilderness, then Katahdin. For the next 100 miles we would not cross any roads, except for an occasional logging road and according to our handbook, "Is some of the most remote-feeling mountains and forest traversed by the Trail. It is suggested that ten days of food be carried through the wilderness although most hikers make it through in less." Midnite's drop box contained two drops in one. She had arranged for Mr. Shaw to meet us halfway through the wilderness, which we would be entering when we left Monson, on an old logging road to deliver five days worth of food so we could avoid carrying the necessary ten days of supplies. By doing this, we would be able to enjoy this last stretch without being burdened by a heavy pack.

Breakfast the next morning lived up to its reputation as Mr. Shaw made his way around the table taking our order. As the aromas of french toast, eggs, home fries, sausage and bacon drove us mad, Mr. Shaw approached each of us, one at at time, with his video recorder asking us to state our trail name and where we were from. We could only imagine how many completed tapes he had tucked away and how honored we felt to become a part of his thru-hiker video library. We finally pushed ourselves away from the table and loaded our gear into Mr. Shaw's truck for a shuttle back to the trail. We lifted our loads to our shoulders, hugged, and said "Next stop, Katahdin!"

We were informed by Mr. Shaw about fording an outlet of a beaver pond that sounded horrible. We had visions of waist high, muddy water and were relieved when it was only mid-calf deep. We had made the ford the previous day in our sandals without any problems and vowed to continue this procedure instead of soaking our boots. Out of Africa won the "wet boot" bet when they finally dried out during our overnight stay at the hostel, so we stopped and strapped on our sandals before entering the cold, murky water. This ford was slightly different than a flowing stream and our feet sank into the mud and had a suction cup hold on us as we tried to lift our legs to take a step. We decided to have an easy day to Leeman Brook Lean-To and completed the 6.3 miles to find McCoy waiting for us when we arrived. She had decided, as we had, to take her time through the wilderness and also wanted to have some company for these last miles as her partner, Morning Glory, jumped ahead from Monson. We were delighted at the prospect of hiking with McCoy. She had a wonderful sense of humor and we really enjoyed her company. McCoy offered to build a small fire as it was a chilly, overcast day, and she much preferred the warmth of the Florida sunshine she was accustomed to. "I'll boil some water for hot chocolate," Out of Africa volunteered, "and that will help warm us up." She had retrieved, from a hiker's box, a ziplock bag full of what we thought was hot chocolate and prepared a cup for McCoy and herself. Midnite had plenty of her own individual packets and opted to use hers and lighten her load the next day by one. As Out of Africa added the hot water to the powder, she commented, "This doesn't look right," as it looked more like lumpy gravy than hot chocolate. We all examined it, and although it tasted chocolaty, we finally concluded that it was chocolate instant pudding, and since food (or in this case, drink) is never wasted by a thru-hiker, it was consumed anyway. Our first day in the wilderness left me looking forward to the days ahead and as McCoy and Out of Africa continued to laugh about their hot pudding, I entered in my journal: "It was so quiet in the woods today. There was no sound of the wind, birds or the rustling of leaves as the squirrels scampered across them. There's usually some kind of noise. It was so beautiful to hear nothing, if that makes sense."

The mornings were becoming cooler, but still warming to the 50's during the day and the hiking was fabulous. The wilderness was everything we expected it to be with the leaves rapidly changing color, ponds dotting the landscape and a welcome change of relatively easy terrain. Little Wilson Falls was spectacular as it plunged 60 feet into the gorge below. The fording continued however, and we approached Big Wilson Stream not quite sure what to expect. It was our widest crossing to date and was only mid-thigh deep and relatively calm. The frigid water made the wider crossings difficult as our feet would instantly go numb and begin to ache up into our ankles. We crossed first without incident and McCoy soon followed and joined us safely on the other side before proceeding to Long Pond Stream for our next feet washing. It seemed to take longer to sit down and take our boots on and off than it did to cross the streams, but Long Pond Stream broke our stride as we searched for a safe crossing. It wasn't as wide as Big Wilson Stream, but it was deeper and the current was much faster. Small rocks on the bottom made footing precarious, and sunlight filtering across the surface made it difficult to see the bottom. It was hard to avoid stepping into the many small holes that lay ready to trap the unwary. The water reached mid-thigh on Out of Africa before she was halfway across. We tried to avoid the areas where the current seemed to be strongest, but it wasn't always possible. It was a bit of an ordeal, but we tried not to dwell on it too much, or think about it until we had to do it. We were always thankful when we were both across safely. Before reaching Long Pond Stream Lean-To, we came across a sign that read: 99 MILES - KATAHDIN, and as near as we could figure, seven days to get there.

We had been enjoying heavenly sunshine the last few days but awoke September 24th to gray skies and the threat of rain. Luckily it held off for us to ride a roller coaster again through Chairback Gap with numerous steep, rocky descents. Just when we thought they were over! We decided to push on an extra 1.7 miles to the West Branch of the Pleasant River which required another ford. We figured it would be easier to get it out of the way instead of dreading it all night and possibly contend with rain if we waited until the next morning. The river was shallow, barely covering our ankles, so we opted to ford barefoot since we were planning to camp on the other side and this would allow our sandals to remain dry. The frigid water brought tears to our eyes. It felt like sticking our feet into giant ice cubes, and holding them there, and we tried to hurry across, but its impossible to move that quick when you can't feel what you're walking on. We emerged anxious to put on our wool socks, pitch the tent and crawl in our sleeping bags, which is exactly what we did. We were returning to the routine of the "early days." Get to camp, eat dinner, and go to sleep. It was becoming too cold to do anything else in the evenings.

I awoke at 4:30 a.m. to the patter of a gentle rain on the rainfly of the tent and even though Out of Africa and I were a bit cramped in her tent, I was in no big hurry to leave my warm surroundings. We finally forced ourselves out into the drizzle and hit the trail. It was a beautiful trail for the first 5 1/2 miles with little elevation change and the rain was tolerable, but things quickly changed, for the worse. Our handbook warned us of White Cap Mountain as being "an exposed rocky summit" and that "blazing is sometimes hard to follow, so be especially alert." Just what we didn't need to know on a cold, and rainy day. We crossed three peaks, each one becoming colder and the fog growing thicker. Before the summit of White Cap Mountain, we gave in and finally stopped for lunch. We tried to eat as fast as we could before our bodies cooled down and we could get moving again, but even 15 minutes was too long. We talked about warm things and Millinocket, but it seemed such a long way off. The summit was to offer us another view of Katahdin, but as usual, we descended once again seeing only fog. We hiked as hard and as fast as our wet bodies would carry us to reach Logan Brook Lean-To. Out of Africa became chilled as soon as we stopped and as always, I had my eye out for signs of hypothermia. I suggested that she put water on to boil for hot chocolate and I would find our water supply for the evening, which I hastily did knowing that something good and hot would be waiting for me when I returned. We quickly added the dry clothing from our packs to our shivering bodies, drank our hot chocolate, then stripped everything off and crawled into our sleeping bags to get warm, pulling the hoods tight to keep the body heat in. Soon the feeling returned to our hands and feet and we would poke our heads out occasionally to see who was shivering their way into the shelter. McCoy arrived and duplicated our efforts and we were soon trying to make the best of it by laughing and joking, but deep down inside we were thinking Bahama's, pizza, hot baths, fuzzy slippers, and flannel sheets. Nights like this made us want to be done NOW, and did not leave us looking forward to getting up the next morning, especially knowing that we had a ford facing us first thing.

What a difference from the day before as we emerged from our bags the next morning, expecting rain, but instead welcomed with the first hint of sunlight. The ford of the

East Branch of Pleasant River was nothing more than rock hopping and we were relieved we didn't have to submerge our feet in the icy water. The temperature climbed to the mid-50's and it was a dream hike past countless ponds as we made our way to Cooper Brook Falls Lean-To. The trail was heavenly with flat easy terrain and no rocks, plus our packs were light as we would be meeting Mr. Shaw the next day to obtain our last food supply. Cooper Brook Falls was another place I had dreamed of while planning my hike, and Out of Africa's and my spirits had improved greatly from the day before as we made our way to the lean-to. Countless nights at home had been spent pouring over the handbook reading the descriptions of all the wonders we would see and experience on our hike, and many, like Cooper Brook Falls remained embedded in my memory. I imagined a peaceful waterfall, winding its way in front of the shelter, surrounded by flat rocks that were warmed by the sun, just waiting for a tired thru-hiker to arrive and rest her weary body. The picture in my mind was exactly what I saw as we approached the shelter, and the warm, inviting rock had my name written all over it. I took a quick "bath" cleaning the mud off of my legs that had been there for two days, (cleanliness was not a priority when it was cold and rainy), then laid my wet gear out to dry while I basked in the warmth and serenity of this place. Kevin and Stephen of the Disciples were at the shelter when we arrived, fixing a late lunch. They were known for taking long lunches, sometimes an hour or more, and arriving late at the shelters in the evening. They were right on course for the day as they would be moving on after their rest. We had been hiking with Kevin, a.k.a. Sissyphus the Happy, since day three of our trek, and we talked of the trail and the magic of it. As they were preparing to leave it suddenly dawned on us that this would probably be the last time we would see Kevin and Stephen. It was scary realizing that in five days and 64 more miles, our journey would be complete, and all of our trail family would be scattered to the far corners of the country. Our thoughts, the remainder of the day, would shift back and forth from thinking of re-entry into the real world and the next journey of our life, and living in the moment. As the sound of the falls serenaded us to sleep, I entered in my journal: "How strange it will be for Out of Africa and me to stand atop Katahdin and know that the next day we won't find out what's on the other side."

We had arranged to meet Mr. Shaw at Jo Mary Road, an old logging road, at 11:00 a.m. and since it was only 3.7 miles from Cooper Brook Falls Lean-To, we figured we might as well try and sleep in and take our time breaking camp, something we rarely did. It had been quite a while since we had hiked on flat terrain and we covered the distance in less than an hour and a half. We thought we were at the wrong road since we got there so quickly, but since there were no other roads on the map, we just sat and prayed that we were at the right place. It was a little unsettling to realize that if he didn't show for some reason, that we would be in a bit of a jam since the food supply in our pack had dwindled to a few granola bars. A few minutes before 11:00 a.m., a car approached carrying our goods and we quickly repacked and set off for Jo Mary Lake. We had passed a southbounder the day before who informed us that there was free food for thru-hikers at Antler's Campsite which was situated along the bank of Jo Mary Lake. We had read in our handbook about "manna from heaven" but there was no explanation as to what that meant. Again, we covered the 4.2 miles in record time and arrived for a late lunch. Alex and Cat, two former thru-hikers, pack in supplies around the same time every year and feed thru-hikers for four to five days, which is quite an undertaking given our appetites. What a feast lay before us as we approached the camp: hamburgers, hot dogs, cheese, crackers, fruit, and they cooked "real" food for breakfast and dinner, not Lipton or instant mashed potatoes, but soup, pork chops, etc. and the standard breakfast fare of pancakes and eggs. I instantly spied a loaf of bread and jelly and toasted numerous slices of bread over the fire, while Out of Africa filled up on hot dogs. It was a real treat to eat on the trail without rationing the amount we could eat. Day after day we ate from our food bags only a certain amount so as not to run out before our next re-supply. We could have quite easily stayed there for days and filled our bellies and the lake was by far the prettiest we had seen since entering Maine. We reluctantly said our goodbyes to Alex and Cat, thanked them for their magic and headed for Potaywadjo Spring Lean-To for the night. We discussed over dinner that night how much we were looking forward to

I believe I'll accomplish what I set out to do. I believe in my strength, my perseverance, my tenacity. I believe in my goals, I am focused, and I am determined.

the creature comforts of the real world, especially since we had been wearing the same pair of socks for six days in a row. (We always kept one pair dry to put on in camp since the weather had turned cold). But still the impending re-entry had us on edge and as much as we wanted to be finished, we also wanted time to slow down.

September 28th. The threat of rain pushed us 18.2 miles to Rainbow Stream Lean-To, the shelter pictured in the 1987 National Geographic article about the trail that also inspired Out of Africa to attempt a thru-hike. We were running into southbounders daily and encouraged them to give it their all and we were glad we were in our shoes and not theirs. We had planned to camp next to Pollywog Stream, but we really didn't fancy breaking down a wet tent in the morning, and we were glad that we pushed on to the lean-to. McCoy was there waiting for us when we arrived and announced that Wildflower was there and was anxious to see us. We hadn't seen her since Pennsylvania and wasn't even sure that she was still on the trail. She had a tough hike through the White Mountains where she took a bad fall and received a slight concussion. Undaunted, she mailed gear ahead and hiked hut to hut while she recuperated, carrying only a day pack. What courage and determination she had and we were thrilled to see her. The shelter and surrounding area quickly filled as one member after another of our trail family arrived, and you could feel the excitement and electricity in the air as we discussed arriving at Katahdin in three days. Most everyone was planning to climb on October 1st, with the exception of some of the male hikers who were going to pull a big mileage day the next day and summit on the 30th of September. Most everyone tented with the exception of McCoy, Pennywise, Troll and us and we were so keyed up that we laid in our bags for quite some time after sunset laughing and joking and having a wonderful time. Oh how we would miss our family members and the shelters at night. With my maglite strapped to my head, as it was every night, I entered in my journal the following: "I told Out of Africa today that I may be teary eyed the next three days; joy, excitement, fear, all rolled into one. I remember thinking before I started the trail that never in my life have I wanted to succeed at anything more than to complete this trip, and Lord willing in three more days, I will. WOW." As the rain began to fall,

I turned off my light and drifted off to sleep, dreaming of Katahdin.

We woke up feeling a little sluggish after our big mileage day and staying up a little later than usual, but at least it wasn't raining as we left the shelter. The trail, however, was saturated and we tiptoed through standing water most of the morning. After 2,130 miles we were STILL trying to keep our feet dry. We were, if nothing else, dedicated! We passed a southbounder that had climbed Katahdin in three inches of snow on September 25th. We were keeping our fingers (and toes) crossed that it would melt by the time we arrived. We gradually climbed to Rainbow Ledges and the sun warmed our bodies as we hurriedly walked along the top. We were (we hoped) finally going to get our first view of Katahdin that was, according to our handbook, "The fourth best view," but we had missed the first three thanks to inclement weather. My mind (as it often did), was somewhere else and surprisingly I was not thinking of Katahdin when out of the corner of my eye I caught a glimpse of what I thought was "our" mountain . It scared me as I wasn't expecting to see it so soon. A few more steps and the trees parted to display the most magnificent mountain I had ever seen. "I see it," I shouted to Out of Africa. "See what?" she questioned. "Katahdin," I tearfully replied. I was in awe. It was so huge and the peak was covered by white fluffy clouds. All I could do was stare at it and cry. I was actually seeing what I had dreamed about for so long. Before our journey started I don't think I ever really thought that I would make it the whole way. I figured I would give up and I never imagined myself standing there staring at Katahdin. It was hard for me to take my eyes off of such majesty, but we were tired and wanted to get to the shelter, so we left, promising to see it again in two more days. The register at Hurd Brook Lean-To is full of thoughts by thru-hikers; those just starting, and those, like us, finishing. How sad it was to be reading our last trail register. We would pass one last shelter before Katahdin Stream Campground, at Daicey Pond, but would not be staying there as was the practice with most thru-hikers, opting instead to continue to the campground at the base of our final climb. We were joined at the shelter by a new group of thru-hikers who we had not met before. They had all been behind us, and of course, knew who we were since they had been reading our register entries since Springer Mountain in Georgia. They were all very strong hikers and we were amazed at the daily average of miles they had been completing in order to catch up with us since most of them started at least three weeks after we did. My journal entry for the night reflected my joy and fear of the day: "My emotions are up and down. I hate to see it end. My body says stop, but my heart says go. I suppose anyone that sees a dream fulfilled as Out of Africa and I are about to do, finds herself at a loss. Where do we go from here? Set new goals and dream new dreams! 18.7 miles to go. I don't suppose I will realize that the hike is over until we are in the car and on our way home."

The last few nights had been sleepless for me and the previous night was no exception. There had been too much on my mind and the adrenalin and excitement wouldn't let my body rest. But, as I told Out of Africa as we stepped from the shelter and were greeted by blue skies, "Soon I will have all the sleep and rest I need. My body is looking forward to it, but I'm not so sure my mind is." Rumors had been flying up and down the trail about the "killer donuts" that were available at the campstore at Abol Bridge, which also marked the end of the 100 Mile Wilderness. The thought of sinking our teeth into a donut the size of a dinner plate, after nine straight days of trail food, was all the motivation we needed to cover the beautifully flat, 3.5 miles in record time. How odd it seemed to hear traffic again as we reached the road. For nine days we heard only the sounds of the forest and the cars were so loud as they flew by us. The peace and solitude we had experienced was quickly swept away as we were introduced once again to the real world. As we crossed the bridge, our eyes fixed on the campstore, we were surprised once again with another breathtaking view of Katahdin. The closer we came to it, the larger it became and we stopped to soak it all in. The donuts could wait. We were soon joined by our shelter mates from the night before and hurried on to satisfy our (always present) hunger. We dropped our packs and threw open the door, our eyes quickly scanned the inside for these gigantic "thru-hiker" donuts. In the corner of the store was a covered tray that we were sure housed these palatable gems, and we approached it licking our lips and ready to dive in. Much to our dismay, the tray was empty: we had beaten the delivery truck which would not arrive for another two hours! We, of course, did find something to pacify us, although it wasn't quite the same. We all made our way back outside to enjoy the sunshine, disappointed, but ready to hit the trail and reach the mountain that was staring down at us. The weather and the trail were magnificent and we were really enjoying the late morning when we came to the junction of Fox and Knowlton Brook and an unexpected ford. It was by far, the worst one yet, and mentally we weren't prepared for it as we thought we were done crossing streams. The best means of crossing was on a log, but after taking a closer look at it, we quickly ruled it out. To reach the wet log we had to hop from a rock to it, and there was no way we were going to attempt that. Wildflower was on the opposite bank and shouted over the roar of the stream, "I didn't cross on the log, I forded where you're standing. The bottom's not too slick, but the current is strong," she continued. We could see that for ourselves and we were growing more uncomfortable by the minute. Midnite volunteered to go first, and after we found another stick to help maintain our balance, we put on our sandals and she stepped from the solid ground of the bank.

Mel: *It started out about mid-thigh deep, but after three steps it dropped quickly and was nearly to my waist. I was quickly losing the feeling in my feet, and although it wasn't a wide stream, I was afraid they would go completely numb before I reached the opposite bank as I was moving very slow. The water crashed against my hips and threw me off balance, and I yelled back to Out of Africa to take her time and be careful of the dropoffs. I was shaking from my head to my white, numb toes from fear and cold as I finally reached the other side and turned to wait for Out of Africa.*

Lindi: *As soon as we took off our boots and socks, I felt we had made a mistake as we watched the water splashing around the large rocks in the stream. Although the log was very slick, and not very stable, I felt we should have crossed on it, but it was my call and I didn't say anything about my doubts to Midnite. She would much rather brave that torrent, than inch her way up the slippery incline of the first log. I could hardly rush back and go across on the log either, I could just see Midnite's face if I did that. With the noise of the raging water, it was almost impossible to hear* *what Wildflower was shouting, but she pointed, and we took it that she was giving us an idea of the way across. We put on our sandals and I watched Midnite slip into the water and wade a few feet. The water was already mid-thigh on her and rose higher as she dropped into a hole. She turned and shouted to be careful. She righted herself, and with the help of another pole, she crossed without mishap. It's always easier watching from the bank, but then it was my turn. I had only gone a few feet, and was bringing my foot up to negotiate a rock, when my sandals came undone. I had to try and fasten them while standing on one leg in the rushing water. I looked up and caught a glimpse of Midnite and Wildflower's anxious faces. I wondered what mine looked like. By now the water was nudging the bottom of my shorts, and then it was ·mid-hip, cold and numbing. It seemed to take a long time to cross, but it couldn't have been more than ten minutes. I pulled myself out on the opposite bank and joined Midnite in a small patch of sunlight. It was definitely cigarette time! Wildflower rubbed my arm, her concern evident on her face. "I was worried about you," she said. "I was worried about myself," I joked, but that was the last ford.*

We decided to stop for lunch and let our feet thaw out and calm our nerves before continuing to Daicey Pond. A little further on, we came across a group of hikers who had passed us at the stream: Dead Man Walking, Mountain Lion, Gypsy and Bandana Light. They were talking and laughing with Skylark who was going the other way! After they went off, we stayed awhile with Skylark. She had made the summit of Katahdin the day before, and was now hiking back to Abol Bridge in the hopes that she would meet up with her friends, The Riders of the Storm, who she hadn't seen for some time. "I may summit again with them," she said. "Are you mad?" we asked, "surely once is enough for anyone" - anyone, except Skylark. She filled us in on what to expect during our climb tomorrow and repeatedly commented, "It was awesome." We hugged and tearfully said our goodbyes before continuing on. We couldn't hike fast enough to Daicey Pond Campground. We came out of the trees and crossed a small parking lot and suddenly there it was - Katahdin, and all the photos we had seen from this vantage point did not do justice to its beauty and strength. Reflecting into the crystal blue waters of Daicey Pond it was as if it spoke to us "Well done, you're almost there, the summit awaits you."

We were required to check in at the ranger station upon our arrival, and we stood around, anxiously awaiting our turn to reserve a shelter at Katahdin Stream Campground, if there were any available. We were disappointed to learn that the last shelter had been reserved by Bert and Ernie, two brothers thru-hiking who we had met for the first time the night before at Hurd Brook Lean-To. Seeing our sullen faces, they offered to share the shelter with us so we would not have to spend our last night on the trail cramped in Out of Africa's tent. We made a brief stop at the Daicey Pond Shelter to read the register and were delighted to see a message from Buzz asking us to call him when we had finished. He was hoping to climb on September 25th and was probably already back at home in North Carolina. The adrenalin was pumping through my body so fast I could barely breathe as we shouldered our packs for the last time. The 2.4 miles from Daicey Pond to Katahdin Stream Campground were glorious. The surrounding peaks, dwarfed by Katahdin, were ablaze with the fall colors, and the sky was a magnificent blue backdrop to them. I was burning film almost as fast as my pulse was beating, and I was pinging off the trees as I continually called to Out of Africa, "There it is again," every time a different view of Katahdin came into sight. We reached the road to the campground and our first stop was to, once again, check in with the ranger. He told us that the weather would be cold for our climb the next day, but dry and sunny, and we should still be prepared for anything. Three days earlier, they would not allow anyone to climb as the summit was covered in ice and snow and no matter what the weather forecast called for, it could change instantly. We were informed that we must sign in before we climbed in the morning, and again when we returned. The shelters at the campground are small and will only accommodate four hikers. We were thankful to Bert and Ernie for offering to share the space with us and we would certainly be warm and cozy on our last night. We had seen McCoy earlier in the day at Abol Bridge and after organizing our gear for the climb, returned to the ranger station to look for her. I had decided that I would carry the day pack I had sent in my Monson maildrop leaving my full pack behind on the porch at the ranger station. Out of

Africa would lighten her load but carry hers to the summit. It was sad to think that I would be leaving my full pack behind, after all it had been as faithful to me as Out of Africa had been, but I didn't want to be burdened down on our last day. McCoy had made her way to the campground by the time we returned and the excitement continued to build as other members of our family made there way in, one at a time: Wildflower, Mountain Lion, Bandana Light, Dead Man Walking, Gypsy, Screamer and Cajun C, and Casper. These would be our climbing partners tomorrow and we were all MORE THAN READY to climb. McCoy came to call after dinner with a special treat that she had packed in from Abol Bridge. Out of Africa had never heard of Jiffy Pop popcorn and McCoy demonstrated the fine art of popping it using the flame from a WhisperLite stove. Despite Out of Africa's arm giving out from shaking it back and forth, we soon had our farewell celebration to the trail underway eating popcorn and drinking warm pink lemonade.

My journal entry was lengthy as there were so many thoughts in my head: "My day pack is ready." "It's hard to believe that tomorrow night we will be in a motel, clean and warm with our feet stretched out on a bed and our journey will be complete. I see my pack hanging on the lean-to wall and my worn out boots beneath it and I can't believe that after tomorrow I won't be putting them both on again. So many memories: the views, our pain, my fall in New York, wanting to leave the trail in Connecticut, the changing of the seasons, so many friends, so many triumphs, so many stories to tell and so many miles walked! My dream is about to be fulfilled and I never imagined it would. I still think sometimes that I am asleep and this is a dream and I'll wake up and still weigh 74 pounds, that its just been a beautiful dream, which it certainly has been. Maybe, tomorrow when I'm standing on top I'll realize I'm wide awake and that dreams really do come true." My body wanted to rest for our final climb the next day, but, as I snuggled into my sleeping bag for the final time, my head would not allow sleep to come.

October 1st, 1996
Mel: *I awoke to the moon and stars shining, and as I exited my sleeping bag at 4:30 a.m., I knew that we would be blessed with blue skies and sunshine. Such a strange*

feeling to load our packs for the last time. How many times had we done that over the last 179 days? At first light, we were ready to climb. We had left my pack and Out of Africa's extra gear at the ranger station and we were the first to sign the climbing register at 6:15 a.m. The trail was beautiful for the first mile, then gradually began to ascend over rocks and the higher we went the tougher it became. We would be gaining 5,000 feet in elevation in four miles. Above treeline we could feel the temperature drop and the wind pick up. We stopped for a break and added another layer of clothing before continuing. We were well above treeline and reached the boulders that Skylark had informed us of and began scrambling up and over them as we had so many times before. At times iron hand holds had been drilled into the rocks to aide us in pulling ourselves up and I couldn't help but think what the descent would be like. For the first time, I wasn't afraid. I kept thinking that everything we had faced on this entire journey had prepared us for this final climb. I could see a false peak above me and it was sheer torture, mentally, trying to imagine what would lie on the other side once I reached it. One thing was for sure, I knew it wasn't the summit, not yet. I couldn't wait to reach that peak and though I continued to climb, I felt as if I was going nowhere. We finally reached it and as I stepped onto level ground, the flat, barren, tableland laid before us and in the distance I could see two peaks, but which one was the summit? Again, I was hiking, but going nowhere as the cold wind swirled around me and we began to see patches of ice and snow, the remains of the storm days earlier. Dead Man Walking suddenly appeared from out of the blue, and passed us saying, "See you at the top." I watched as his body became smaller and the distance between us grew. I followed the direction he was going and felt we were taking the long way around to get there, but we continued to follow the white blazes that had brought us this far. We ascended gradually and at last our dream was a reality. The sign I had seen in my dreams for so many months finally came into view and I stopped and turned towards Out of Africa. "I can see it" I yelled as the tears streamed down my cheeks. I waited for her to reach me, took her hand in mine and we walked the last few hundred yards, side by side, just as we had in spirit for the last six months. I expected to reach the top and scream at the top of my lungs, "We made it." Instead I embraced Out of Africa, and sobbing uncontrollably, whispered, "We Did It." I didn't want the moment to end. I wanted to hold on to it, and Out of Africa forever. I walked to the sign, leaned over and gently kissed it, fulfilling the promise I had made 179 days earlier at Springer Mountain. It was 10:05 a.m., five minutes later than when we left Springer Mountain on April 5th. We had made a sign in Monson that read: "I Said I'd Try It, I Did It, And It's Done." This quote was changed slightly from what Grandma Gatewood (one of our inspirations) said after her first thru-hike: "I Said I'd Do It, I Did It, And It's Done." We never said "We'd Do It," only that "We'd Try," and what pride we felt as we each took turns holding it for our picture to be taken next to the weather beaten sign that read: "Katahdin Northern Terminus of the Appalachian Trail." McCoy and our other family members soon joined us at the summit, each fulfilling their own dreams as hugs, tears and photographs welcomed each of them. The wind and cold began to chill us, but before we turned our backs to the summit and began our descent, we each retrieved our stone that we had carried from Springer Mountain, and placed it ceremoniously at the base of the sign. How odd it was to walk South and leave the next mountain range unexplored. As we began our descent, we proudly announced "Today We Are Thru-Hikers."

Lindi: We woke early on a bright, clear morning, still dark with a cold, silver moon and sprinkling of stars. Midnite was already rustling around, and it was only 5:00 a.m.! My flashlight batteries had died the night before, and I had to grope around in the dark. A friend of Midnite's had told her, "You don't need a flashlight until you turn it on." That's true and I didn't suspect I had lost a contact lens until we reached the ranger station where we were leaving our gear while we climbed the mountain. I kept closing my eye, and in the end decided that I had lost a lens. I thought I would wear my glasses, but when I fished them out of my pack, the small screw that secures the arm was missing and as a consequence, the lens had dropped out. I couldn't wear my glasses, and would have to climb Katahdin with only one contact lens. As we began to climb I quickly forgot about it. It didn't seem to make much difference, and I could see quite well. We were the first on the trail, and the mountain rose daunting before us. The sun was shining and it was an easy climb until just past the tree line. After that, things became a little tougher. The rocks were more exposed, and in some places, the wind caught us and tore at our clothes and packs. A huge spine of rocks, like massive stepping stones, led upwards. Some had iron bars for hikers to pull themselves up with, others had no foot or hand holds, and we scrambled our way up. We were at the top of what I thought was the summit, and saw that a vast plateau spread before us. Ice still lay amongst the rocks. We had made it this far, perhaps Paloma, the guardian spirit of the mountain, would let us reach the summit. Dead Man Walking and Mountain Lion passed us and were soon lost to our sight. They appeared silhouetted against the skyline - they seemed so small. Midnite stopped and waited for me, holding out her hand. We walked the rest of the way together. Laughing and crying, we hugged and looked around. It was very cold, and we could see for miles. The sky was washed with soft white clouds. It was a perfect day. We had achieved our goal. We had walked 2,159 miles. It was done.

The descent was not nearly as difficult as we had expected it to be and we stopped halfway down for lunch. McGyver, unexpectedly, passed us and we watched as he began his climb up the false peak we had labored over a few hours earlier. It amazed us how much steeper it appeared looking at it from that vantage point and with someone climbing up it. We were lucky not to have witnessed that before we climbed. The remainder of the hike back to the campground was quiet as we both reflected on the day, still not believing that shortly we would truly be finished. We were both looking forward to soaking our aching bodies in a warm tub and giving our trail weary legs a much needed rest. Despite the rigors of the trail, we both knew that after a few days of creature comforts we would be ready to hit the trail again - or would we? The fear and anticipation we felt at Springer Mountain returned as we completed the last of our five million steps.

We signed in at the trail register, and proceeded to the campground to wait for McCoy who was close behind us. We walked up to a picnic table, dropped our packs and looked over our shoulders at the mountain of our dreams.

One by one our trail family filed down from the mountain and we lingered in the shadow of "our" mountain, not wanting to leave. After tearful goodbyes to our friends, we reluctantly picked up our packs and made our way to the road that would lead us to Millinocket. We held out our thumbs for the last time and were soon picked up by a gentleman and his son who offered to drive us the 20 miles to town. He was uncertain where the lodge was that Midnite's mother had reserved rooms for us, but assured us he would find it. He pulled in front of a cafe that was operated by the owner of the lodge and we noticed a sign for it a bit further up the street. We told him we would walk the rest of the way, and as we were thanking him for his kindness we heard a car horn blow behind us. We turned to see Midnite's mother, father, and brother-in-law pulling in. Arrangements had been made, during our re-supply in Monson, for them to meet us October 2nd in Millinocket. This would allow us an extra day to climb Katahdin if the weather was bad. They decided to surprise us and arrive a day early. Not finding us at the lodge, they were heading for Katahdin, searching for us in every car they passed. Luckily, there is only one road into town. Midnite's mother spotted us and they quickly turned around and followed us back to town. What a joyous reunion we had in the middle of main street.

Mel: *I was so glad my family came to meet us a day early. I had been secretly hoping that they would, and knowing my parents the way I do, I expected to see tham at Katahdin. They were such an important part of my journey and it meant so much to me that they were there to celebrate our completion. My mother threw her arms around my neck, kissed my cheek, and said, "I missed you so much, BOY DO YOU SMELL!" She always has been an honest woman!*

We quickly showered and were treated to a magnificent dinner by Midnite's parents. It was a beautiful ending to a glorious day as we retired to our warm, cozy room. The fears of the "real world" would be dealt with tomorrow - for tonight, as we closed our eyes, our minds replayed the image of us - hands clasped and hiking sticks raised, standing atop the mountain of our dreams.

I don't wish for you a pot of gold at the end of the rainbow but happiness at the end of the trail
Midnite's mother

EPILOGUE

Tomorrow we would begin our next adventure as we started our journey home. Home - such a strange sound. The trail has been our home for so long now. How will we readjust? We can only hope that we remember all of the lessons the trail has taught us as we start our lives over again: Patience is needed in today's hurry up world and we must remember to take one day at a time, just as we took one mile at a time.

We are finished. We won't be hiking tomorrow or the next day, but we will always be together in spirit and in each other's hearts. Our journey of friendship will always continue.

God of the hills and our Guide on the upward climb, give us vision and strength for our journey through life. When the trail becomes faint and mist hides the summit, show us the way; when the path is rough with sharp stones as it winds around the jagged cliffs, take our hands and lead us; and when we near the summit and the deep chasms drop abruptly on either side, keep our steps firm and sure. Then at the end of the journey bring healing to our bruised feet and ease our tired muscles and may we hear you say, "Well done, you have reached the summit of the hills of your God."

ACKNOWLEDGEMENTS

The authors would like to thank so many people for so many things:

Melody (Midnite):

My family, for ALL of your love, support, encouragement, the miles you traveled to see us and for walking all 2,159 miles with me. I could not have asked for a better support team. **My friends**, Mimi and Jenny for encouraging me to take the first step and standing by me in spirit for the five million that followed, and for the use of your computer, futon and fire. **My supporters** in my hometown of Marietta, Ohio. Your prayers, cards and letters carried me many miles. All of the **trail volunteers** who put in many hours of hard work keeping the trail maintained for all to enjoy. All of the **"trail angels"** that blessed us with their magic. **Dan 'Wingfoot' Bruce**, author of "The Thru-Hiker's Handbook," for allowing us to reprint excerpts from his book. **Cindy Carbone**, for her expertise in editing this book. God, for giving me a second chance on life, leading me to the trail, and protecting me. And of course, **Out of Africa**, my partner, my friend, who made the journey much more than a hike. I couldn't have done it without you. Our partnership was a match made in heaven.

Lindi (Out of Africa):

Des, for your love, encouragement and help, even though you knew I would be gone for seven months. **My mother** who never missed a maildrop. **My family and friends** for their interest and letters. **Mimi**, for a quiet place to work and for the loan of Ziggy and Bucky. **The trail volunteers**, without their work, there would be no trail. **My adopted American family**, who treated me like a member of their family, and for their unfailing support. And **Midnite**, my partner, friend and trail companion - my thanks for everything you did for me, and are still doing.

THE HOUSE ON OUR BACK

<u>Midnite's Gear</u>
Gregory Palisades Plus Backpack
Eureka Cirrus 2 Tent
Moonstone Shasta 0 Degree Sleeping Bag (cooler months)
Slumberjack 30 Degree Sleeping Bag (warmer months)
Ridgerest 3/4 Sleeping Pad
Sweetwater Guardian Water Filter

Scorpion II Propane/Butane Stove
Propane/Butane Fuel Canisters (2)
1 - 1 quart stainless steel cook pot & lid
Lexan cup
1 spoon
pot grippers
water sack
2 - 1 quart water bottles

First Aid Kit (band-aids, moleskin, first-skin, second skin, antibiotic, anti-itch cream)
Journal
Small Radio (hooked on to sternum strap of pack)
Canon SureShot Camera and film
Small Swiss Army Knife
Maglite and extra batteries

Vasque Clarion II Gore Tex Boots - 2 pair
Gore-Tex Rain Parka and Pants
Duofold lightweight jacket
Mid-weight tights (cooler months)
Shorts
Hiking Bra
T-Shirt
Glove and Glove Liners (cooler months)
Polypropylene long-sleeved shirt (cooler months)
Wool/Polypropylene blend socks - 2 pair
Polypropylene sock liners - 3 pair
Fleece headband (cooler months)
Ankle gaiters

Wooden hiking stick

Out of Africa's Gear
Backpacker - Canyon Design 650 Backpack
Sierra Design Clip Flashlight Tent
First Ascent Grey Wolf 0 Degree Down Sleeping Bag
Therm-a-Rest 3/4 mattress
Sweetwater Guardian Water Filter

MSR WhisperLite International Stove
1 - fuel bottle
1 - 1 quart aluminum cookpot
plastic cup
1 spoon
water sack
2 - water bottles
Camp suds

First Aid Kit
Journal
Small Radio
Basic Swiss Army Knife
Maglite

Hi-Tec PCL Boots (1st 500 miles)
Asolo (leather medium weight boots) - 2 pair
Marmot Rain Jacket
Patagonia Rain Pants
Patagonia capilene long underwear and zip undershirt
Shorts
Hiking Bra
T-Shirt
Bandanas - 2

Gloves
Wool socks - 3 pair
Sock liners - 3 pair
Wool hat

Ankle gaiters

Aluminum hiking pole

FOOD FOR MIDNITE'S MAILDROPS
- 75 - Lipton Rice and Pasta Dinners
- 120 - Oatmeal Packets
- 300+ - Granola bars
- 80 - Nutra Grain bars & Pop Tarts
- 100+ - Packaged drinks (Kool-Aid, Crystal Light)

FOOD DEHYDRATED FOR MAILDROPS
- 18#'s - Turkey & Chicken
- 77 cans - Vegetables (Peas & Carrots)
- 250+ cans - Fruit (Peaches, Pineapple, etc.)
- 78 - Fruit roll-ups